The Power of
FASTING And
PRAYING

Getting in Touch with the real You

Apostle. Dr. P.W. Reed, Ph.D.

Unless otherwise indicated, all scriptural quotations are taken from the King James Version of the Bible. All direct quotations from the King James Version are italicized and bold.

Apostle. Dr. P.W. Reed, Ph.D.

The Power of Fasting and Prayer
Getting In Touch With the Real You
Copyright © 2001 by Apostle, Dr. P.W. Reed, Ed.D.
Put Oil of Joy Empowerment, Inc.
Oil of Joy, Inc.
P.O. Box 308
Atlanta, GA. 30096
(678) 796-8013

All rights reserved. No portion of this book may be reproduced or transmitted in any form without the written permission of the publisher.

Published by: Power that Impact lives
ISBN number - 978-0-9998412-5-1

Apostle. Dr. P.W. Reed, Ph.D.

Apostle. Dr. P.W. Reed, Ph.D.

Acknowledgments

The Power of Fasting and Prayer is dedicated to my wife, Toyja N. Reed, my daughter, Dominique N. Reed and Oil of Joy Empowerment, Inc.. This book was written for the exclusive purpose of teaching Christians that there is a way to put on a Christ-like disposition and to exemplify the power of Christ. Yes, Pentecost was the birth of the New Testament Church, but as we will explore, those at Pentecost did not receive the power of the Holy Ghost by watching someone that possessed it, and saying, "I believe I should have what they have." No, in order for them to have received the Holy Ghost with power, they had to tarry for it until it was manifested.

The **Power of Fasting and Prayer** will not only teach Christians how to fast for spiritual and natural results, but how to destroy every yoke of bondage upon his/her own personal life. Fasting is not as hard to do as some have made it seem; however, the mindset of a person who fasts must change and his/her motives behind fasting must be appropriately driven. These and many other issues will be discussed in this book.

People across the nation are professing Christianity and claim to have aspirations of becoming like Christ; however, many people do not want to put up a sacrifice. Christ walked a perfect life before all those He ministered to, healed, and set free. The word of God says, *"For he hath made him to be sin for us, who knew no sin; that we might be made the righteousness of God in him" (II Cor. 5:21)*. Jesus knew what it was to overcome, and has consequently, given us the greatest example. As He overcame the world, He has given us power to do the same, and overcome our adversary, Satan. Let us take a closer look and find out how we will win the battle of the flesh.

PREFACE :
How I Remember

I can remember so clearly, as if it were yesterday. From the age of six years old until eighteen, reared in New Orleans, LA., in a traditional Baptist Church, singing in the choir, sitting on the second pew of the church, I anticipated something miraculous happening that would cause the church to be on fire. As I went back, not out personal desire, but because I had no choice, it was a requirement of my mother that I and my two sisters attend church weekly. I realized my expectation for a powerful move of God was not going to happen. No one in the family knew it, but I would get on my knees and pray nightly before going to bed and one day something miraculous happened.

While praying, I had a vision of myself flying in the air, rising, falling, and surpassing the fowls of the air. I wondered how I could fly when it completely went against anything I had ever witnessed or seen happen to anyone. I did not reveal this vision to anyone in the beginning, because I did not want to be considered the crazy kid. To my dismay, it happened repeatedly, and I began to have dreams and visions. I was so astonished, that I could no longer keep it to myself, so I shared my dreams with my mother. She did not understand most of it and told me she would take me to our pastor. My pastor articulated "that boy has serious problems, thinking God is showing him all those things."

Apostle. Dr. P.W. Reed, Ph.D.

As time went on, I lived a normal life, like any other child, but my sisters would say, "Watch what you say in front of him, because he is different."

Time prevailed, and I began to understand that the parties were becoming mundane, the women were getting a bit inordinate, and what the world had to offer was not the answer. My mother was completely worn out from worrying about me, and at the age of seventeen, she said "enough is enough: it's time for you to get out if you want to be a man, get out of my home". I could not find any friends to turn to. I drove up and down the highway in my 1974 Chevy Malibu, looking for refuge, or someone to turn to, but I could find no one. I found myself lost in anger, but it did not help my situation. I slept in the back of my car for a month and after several weeks, I moved to my grandmother's house. There were uncles and aunts living there, but grandmother did not mind helping. I will never forget the tears that ran down my face, but it was not enough for me to give up the world.

Four weeks had gone by, and I realized I could not live in grandmother's home any longer with uncles and relatives. It was time for me to change things. I found a job and got a cost-effective apartment, which was so small that if you lost something, all you had to do was look down and there it would be. Now I had gotten myself a job, an apartment, enrolled in the Southern University of New Orleans, and things appeared to have been going well. No sooner than that, I met a young lady, who was going to play an important part in changing my life, although I didn't even ask for her help.

Things began to turn for the worst. While I was leaving my job, bullets were flying, which caused me to take a closer look at myself. I had never gotten sick, but now I was in bed sick. I lost my job at the restaurant, my attitude was bad, and I loved fighting anyone that would look at me strangely. The young lady, who I met, did not want me around anymore, and I was not so popular all of a sudden. There was no money in my pockets, and oh, how it seemed all hope was gone! Where was I going to run? What was I going to do? Whom would I turn to? I turned to older women that found me attractive and gave me large sums of money, clothes, and sex.

The young lady that I met on campus invited me to a revival meeting. All I could think about was blowing off my anger in a weight room, and the possibility this was the answer I needed. Nearly three weeks had gone by since I was invited to the month long tent revival. Finally one night a friend of mine, and I were on our way to weight train when suddenly as we were making our way to the door, something happened to me. My desire to pursue bodybuilding left, and instead, my friend and I went to the tent revival. As I sat under that big red, white and blue tent, I listened to a message being preached about Noah and the last days by Evangelist Oscar Lange, a message I will never forget. Tears began to run down my eyes as I sat in amazement listening to the preacher minister the gospel. I ran to the altar, with repentance in my heart and gave my life to the Lord. I joined the church; however, doctrinally some things I was taught did not sit well in my spirit. I asked the pastor for clarification and I was denied that opportunity and was told I was confused. I wanted to know was the truth about God's word. I had never seen in the bible where it was wrong to drink caffeine or to get married with a watch, or foods that God had cleansed no man should call common or unclean. Therefore, I left that branch of the church because there was no clarity.

After I had been saved for three months, the Lord revealed to me a little church, with only a few people worshipping there, which would be my place of spiritual refuge. I joined that ministry, which was born out of the A. A. Allen Revival Ministries. Upon joining, I sat down with my pastor and shared with him the visions I had seen. God had blessed him with the gift of interpretation, so he understood clearly. My calling to preach the gospel was soon prophesied, and yes I rejected it. I did not act on my calling to minister the word of

God until He revealed it to me Himself. My father in the gospel was now going to baptize the entire church and requested we all fast seven days. We were instructed not to eat nor drink anything, other than sips of spring water when the body felt weak.

How well I remember the seventh day of my fast I received my own personal revelation of Jesus Christ. While on my knees praying, I had fallen into a trance. My spirit left my body and it began to ascend towards heaven; yet, I saw myself still on my knees praying while my spirit rose. The speed began to pick up until I was traveling extremely fast, when suddenly I experienced the greatest revelation of my life. The sky appeared to have opened; I realize it was heaven, and the glory of God shined round about me. The voice of God spoke and said, "Son I have chosen you to be a prophet, preach to all nations, languages, and tongues. You are going to prophesy and preach to those that have been wounded, hurt, prostituted, and those that have lived a life of immorality." I began to cry, as the voice spoke, and I covered my face. God spoke to me and told me to go and do what He had chosen for me to do, and all I said was, "God I want to stay right here with you." The Lord told me He had chosen me as prophet, for this hour. In addition, He revealed to me I would lay hands on the sick and they would recover, as well as preach the acceptable year of His coming. I would fast and pray and yokes would be destroyed on the lives of those He instructed me to preach the gospel to.

I believe fasting is the resource that is needed for anyone to discover their true godly potential, to ward off Satan and his angels, and to fight the good fight of faith. Paul said: ***"I beseech you therefore, brethren, by the mercies of God, that ye present your bodies a living sacrifice, holy, acceptable unto God, which is your reasonable service" (Rom. 12:1).***

While I was instructed to fast, I remember how afraid I was and thought I might die fasting. I soon realized fasting was the secret to

"Power, Deliverance, Healing and Miracles". If I only knew, I would get delivered from lust, anger, selfishness, fighting, rebellion, I would have fasted prior to being told by my pastor. Fasting became and yet still is, a vital part of my reasonable service. I believe that fasting is the resource for anyone to discover their true godly potential, to ward off Satan and his angels, and to fight the good fight of faith. Paul pleaded with Christians to give their bodies to God in a sacrificial manner, because there was no longer the sacrifice of animals. He pointed out that when we think of all of the things the Lord has done for us, is fasting too much to ask of a child of God? If you do not want to emulate the ways of the world, let God transform you by the way you think. Fasting is the beginning of your transformation process. Your thoughts will change, your attitude, ungodly ways, and every yoke will be destroyed.

CONTENTS

Acknowledgments v
PREFACE : How I Remember.. vi

Chapter - 1: **Understanding Fasting and Its True Purpose**......... 13
    What Is Fasting?... 13
    You Will Suffer! 17
    What is the True Purpose?... 23

Chapter - 2 : **Misconceptions about Fasting**................................ 29
    The Way It Is 31
    Revival Comes Through Fasting... 33

Chapter - 3 **Preparation** 41
    Getting Your Heart and Mind Right 42
    Fasting Preparation.. 43
    Get Prayed Up! 44
    Study To Be Approved 47
    Clean It Up! 49
    Keep the Pep in Your Step 51

Chapter - 4 **The True Purpose** 55
    Fasting as a Resource 55
    A Heart of Gold 61
    I Can Have A Baby Too! 62
    Cigarettes Won't Bind Me 63
    Clothed In His Right Mind 64
    I Can Sleep Again 65
    What can Happen if I Fast Properly? 65
    30 Spiritual Reasons Why We Should Fast 67
    27 Reasons to Fast for Physical Results 70

Chapter - 5 **Developing a Relationship with God** 73
    Joshua's Relationship with God 74
    Humility is the Key- Abraham 76
    Esther Remembers 79
    Hannah it's Your Time... 82
    "Speak Lord Thy Servant Heareth"................................... 83

Chapter - 6	**Oh, Yes! They Will Change** 85
	Let's Change a Nation 85
	Here He Comes, but Don't Run 87
	Someone Is On Our Side 90
	Favor of God 94
	The Man of God Is a Judge 96
	Ezra's Journey 97
Chapter - 7	**Godly Impact** 99
	It's Time to Fight Back 101
	How to Pray and Not FAINT 102
Chapter - 8	**His Power Is Alive** 109
	Fasting Touches the Heart of God 109
	Jesus Touched the Father 114
	Mary Come Out, the Master's Here! 117
Chapter - 9	**Let's Break Out with Power** 123
Chapter - 10	Can I Make a Difference? 127
	You Can Make a Difference 130
	Daniel Made a Difference 133
	The Kingdom is Restored 138
Chapter - 11	**Not Without a Fight** 145
	The True Apostolic Anointing 145
Chapter - 12	**When a Man Knows to Do Good** 151
	God Spoke To Me! 156
	Don't Let Anything Stop You ! 157
	It's Not Supposed to Be Easy; It's a Challenge! 159
	That Spirit Wants Your Home 161
	When The Lord Speaks 162
	911- A State Of Emergency 163

Chapter - 1

Understanding Fasting and Its True Purpose

What Is Fasting?

We have heard much talk of fasting, and many people do it for many different reasons, but what is fasting all about? Some may look at it as a time to go without something they enjoy, or to say "no" to that which the flesh truly desires, or maybe to not talk on the phone for an hour. In truth, fasting is the denial of the flesh, it was ordained by God for spiritual reasons. The twenty first century is now here, and some will not smoke for an hour, eat for a day, and maybe not swear for a week, calling that a fast. The Lord told Isaiah, 58:3, Behold in the day of your fast you seek your own pleasure, and oppress all your workers. You fast to quarrel and to fight and to hit with a wicked fist. This is not the fast that God has ordained.

Webster's Dictionary defines fasting as:

1. To abstain from all or certain foods, as in observing an holy day;
2. To eat very little or nothing.

The church defines it through the eyes of the scriptures. Paul said, ***"I beseech you therefore brethren, by the mercies of God, that ye present your bodies a living sacrifice, holy, acceptable unto God, which is your reasonable service. And be not conformed to this world but be ye transformed by the renewing of your mind, that ye may prove what is that good, and acceptable, and perfect, will of God." (Rom. 12:1-2)***

Fasting is the process of self-denial. Fasting brings the believer into a closer relationship with God. God's reasonable service to us was to give His only begotten son Jesus at a time when man was destitute, hurting, dying, lawless, and disobedient. Christ died for us not when we were perfect, but yet while we were sinners. Our God given purpose is to give ourselves back to Him. Fasting becomes that spiritual link that brings the believer closer to God. In other words, Paul was saying that it is the least you can do for God to prove your sincerity, and in proving it, you the believer will reap the rewards.

Fasting is the yoke destroyer that gives the Christian common ground with God. When a person fasts, he is taking control of his flesh, telling it, I'm tired of you being in control, and I am going to do something about you because you are not the boss and at times you get out of control. The flesh acts on our senses, will, emotions, and desires many things that it sees, touches, smell, tastes or even hears. It is fact when souls come to the Lord, they should come as they are; however, after they come they should make drastic changes. David said, ***"Behold I was shapen in iniquity; and in sin did my mother conceive me" (Ps. 51:5).***

Because we were born in sin and formed in iniquity, sin was all we knew. If a baby comes out the womb of a parent that speaks only Spanish, that child will speak Spanish, unless he is trained to speak another language. There are parents who have used cocaine or crack frequently; therefore, when the baby comes out of the womb of the mother, he will be referred to as a crack baby. Until repentance came, we were all sinners, and had to learn the newness of life.

There is therefore now no condemnation to them which are in Christ Jesus, who walk not after the flesh, but after the Spirit. For the law of the spirit of life in Christ Jesus hath made me free from the law of sin and death. For what the law could not do in that it was weak through the flesh, God sending his own Son in the likeness of sinful flesh, and for sin, condemned sin in the flesh. That the righteousness of the law might be fulfilled in us, who walk not after the flesh, but after the Spirit. For they that are after the flesh do mind the things of the flesh; but they that are after the Spirit the things of the Spirit. For to be carnally minded is death; but to be spiritually minded is life and peace. Because the carnal mind is enmity against God: for it is not subject to the law of God, neither indeed can be. So then they that are in the flesh cannot please God. (Rom. 8:1-8)

In order for the Christian not to be condemned, he/she must be in Christ. For us to be in Christ we must:

- ☦ Repent and confess Christ as Lord and Savior
- ☦ Baptized (born again)
- ☦ Become spirit filled
- ☦ Follow the example of Christ, doing exactly what He did.

When these things are done, you will become part of the family of God, however, let us talk about remaining a child of God. The word of God is not talking to the sinner about not walking in the flesh, but to the believer. The unbeliever is already walking in the flesh, whether he would agree or not. As seen in 1 Timothy 5:6, *"**she that liveth in pleasure is dead yet while she liveth.**"* In order for us not to walk in the flesh, the flesh must die! What do I mean about the flesh dying?

"Mortify (put to death) therefore your members which are upon the earth, fornication, uncleanness, inordinate affection, evil concupiscence, and covetousness, which is idolatry: For which things sake the wrath of God cometh upon the children of disobedience. In the whch ye also walked some time, when ye lived in them." (Col. 3:5-6)

Since Christ died, our real life, which He has ordained for us has been hidden in Him. The Christian's ultimate goal should be to put heavenly priorities into daily practice. The bible teaches us to not to worry about anything, but to pray about everything (Matthew 6:25). You cannot mortify the deeds of the flesh if you are not willing to be honest with yourself at conversion. If you tell God where you are weak and you truly want help in your weakest areas, He is willing to help you. When this is done, you will experience God's peace, which normal intellect cannot comprehend.

The child of God should put to death the sinful nature and learn how to live in the spirit. Just like a tumor, or a diseased limb on a tree, the practice of sexual immorality, impurity, lust, shameful desires, greed and filthy communication, must be rooted out of the core, before it destroys you. If immoral behavior is lurking inside you, and you are not seeking to kill it out, it will be impossible to please God.

Let us understand that when a sinner accepts Christ, he is a sinner that is saved by grace, and is accustomed to committing sin. That person had never known the way of righteousness, so there must be a renewing of mind and spirit. Christ came, and He made us free through the sacrifice of Himself, but we must do what it takes in order to stay free. Those that walk after the flesh may not agree that they are in the flesh. Some Christians believe everything they do is spirit, and you cannot tell them otherwise or make them believe differently. Only through the word of God we can see our ways and understand that our ways are not like the ways of God. We have all been born in sin and shape in iniquity. We were born into a sinful world and are susceptible to do things that are of the world, due to our sinful nature we possessed from birth.

The Bible declares, *"There is therefore now no condemnation to them which are in Christ Jesus, who walk not after the flesh but after the spirit"* **(Rom. 8:1).** When we have been made free, through the veil of His body, we are no longer held guilty of death. If it had not been for the atonement of Jesus Christ we would be on death row, sentenced to die. Although the Lord has freed us, we must do more than just going to church, in order to stay free. It will take more than reading your bible. Fasting is the course that all Christians should take, because it gives the believer a spiritual edge over Satan's demonic forces. Since fasting is so powerful, Satan tries everything in his power to stop us from fasting. He knows it will destroy the desire for sin.

You Will Suffer!

"Yea, and all that will live godly in Christ Jesus shall suffer persecution." (2 Timothy 3:12)

From that time forth began Jesus to show unto his disciples, how that he must go unto Jerusalem, and suffer many things of the elders and chief priests and scribes, and be killed; and be raised again the third day. Then Peter took him, and began to rebuke him, saying, 'Be it far from thee, Lord: this shall not be unto thee.' But he turned, and said unto 'Peter, Get thee behind me, Satan: for thou savorest (say) not the things that be of God, but those that be of men.' (Matt. 16:21-21)

As a Christian there are going to be many things you will suffer, and you will not have answers to why you are experiencing some of your trials. When Jesus shared with His disciples the suffering He would go through, they could not understand or handle it. The word of God says it was "from that time forth," which suggests He would do it again on future occasions (See Matt. 17:22-23; 20:18). That statement marked a turning point in Jesus's ministry, this emphasis became His death and ressurection. The disciples were with Him but did not understand His true purpose. "For the purpose of the Son of God was manifested, that he might destroy the works of the devil" (1 John 3:8). The child of God must also realize that our purpose is to live for God, help to usher others to Christ and do away with the works of the flesh.

Job was a perfect and upright man in his day; however, his oxen, servants, sheep, camels, and his sons and daughters were destroyed. Job made a profound statement that preachers and teachers quote. He said, ***"Naked came I out of my mother's womb, and naked shall I return thither: the Lord gave, and the Lord hath taken away: blessed be the name of the Lord" (Job. 1:2***1). It is very hard for me to conceive that while God had blessed Job, He also cursed him. Job spoke what his heart was feeling. The Bible lets us know that, ***"for he that cometh to God must believe that he is, and that he is a rewarder of them that diligently seek him" (Heb. 11:6).*** My point is, Job was a believer, and because he was, God would deliver him. He also proved his faithfulness and went through his trial without sinning. It is verifiable Job went through many things, but we understand that what God has blessed, He does not curse. It is God's good pleasure to see His people blessed, but He wants us to do what it takes to keep the blessings flowing. God is not a God that will curse His people, unless His people curse themselves. The apostle John wrote to Gaius, a fellow servant of God, ***"Beloved I wish above all things that thou mayest prosper and be in health, even as thy soul prospereth" (III John 2).*** Therefore, as the soul increases, become built up, learn more, put God first, then God wants us to prosper in all things.

Blessed is the man that endureth temptation: for when he is tried, he shall receive the crown of life, which the Lord hath promised to them that love him. Let no man say when he is tempted, I am tempted of God: for God cannot be tempted with evil neither

tempteth he any man: but every man is tempted when he is drawn away of his own lust, and enticed. Then when lust hath conceived, it bringeth forth sin: and sin, when it is finished, bringeth forth death. (James 1:12-15)

God blesses people who are patient, and will endure their test. At times when people are tested they desire someone to deliver them from their test, not knowing that when the test is theirs, it must be passed. There are times God will remove the hands of people so you can go through it and seek His face. When there is lack we have great opportunity to seek God through fasting. Only after successful completion, you will receive the prize. All Christians will not receive natural prosperity here on earth, but you can rest assure that if you are truly a child of God, you will receive the goal of eternal life for winning the race. Temptation does not come from God; however, it comes from the ungodly desires in our hearts and Satan. The best way to stop temptation is not to entertain it at all, and mortify the desire.

God did not destroy Job's oxen, servants, cattle, or children; God permitted Satan to touch all that Job owned, but without harming him physically. Let us not blame the death of Job's children on God or the Devil, because Job's children were disobedient, and their days were shortened. God is not in evil; neither does He tempt man with evil (James 1:13).

What occurs in similar situations is that people speak what they think or heart feels and not always what the spirit of God directs. Fasting gives us the spiritual understanding and advantage which we might not have had prior to our seeking God. The flesh is always lusting against the spirit, even when we do not recognize it. Children of God, we must understand that ***"the flesh lusteth against the Spirit, and the Spirit against the flesh: and these are contrary the one to the other: so that ye cannot do the things that ye would" (Gal. 5:17).*** Therefore, you may indeed mean well, but if the flesh is not destroyed or put under subjection, your flesh will act up and gravitate to things it should not have.

Then saith Jesus unto them, 'All ye shall be offended because of me this night: For it is written; I will smite the shepherd, and the sheep of the flock shall be scattered abroad. But after I am risen again, I will go before you into Galilee.' Peter answered and said unto him, though all men shall be offended because of thee, yet will I never be offended. Jesus said unto him, 'verily I say unto thee, that this night, before the cock crow, thou shall deny me thrice.' Peter said unto him, though I should die with thee, yet will I not deny thee, likewise also said all the disciples. (Matt. 26:31-35)

When Peter spoke this to Jesus, it sounded well, and I believe he truly meant what he said. However, if he were not in his place at the time when the tempter came, he would fall, lie or even deny. Peter denied Christ, but it did not mean that he was not saved. It just meant that at the moment he was tried, he was not prepared to handle his accusers. If he had been consecrated, he might not have denied Christ.

As we have noticed through the word of God, the intent of the believer may indeed be well, but if he does not become consecrated, there may arise things out of him that will shame the body of Christ. When a person is praying and fasting, he cannot faint. However, when he is not praying and fasting, he will faint. Understanding the word of God, gives you an edge, but putting the word to action, gives you a greater advantage. The Devil hates when the members of the body of Christ put up a sacrifice to lie all night in prayer and supplications before God. The Devil begins to quiver because he knows that you are ready to go to war. Fasting helps you to spiritually mount up for any battle you might face. It is a source of power that benefits the soul as a carbohydrate or a protein drink benefits the body of a bodybuilder. There was nothing ever wrong with the law; we just could not keep the law. It is not hard being a Christian if you are obedient, but if you are disobedient, Christianity will be difficult. If any man calls upon the name of the Lord, he shall be saved. Yet, what is he being saved from? Is he being saved from trouble, adversities, and afflictions? This type of salvation is not in reference to eternal salvation, but to deliverance at that moment. If the person is calling upon the name of the Lord for salvation, yes, of course he can be saved, but he must carry out a few things: (1) fear God, for it is the beginning of knowledge (Prov. 1:7), (2) work out his soul salvation with fear and trembling in the sight of God (Phil. 2:12), (3) never turn back to his old ways, and (4) fast, to keep continue in the right direction.

If we say we want to be like Jesus, we must do what He did. To a large degree, the church has gotten away from God's ordained fast, but it was never the plan of God not to fast. *__Then was Jesus led up of the Spirit into the wilderness to be tempted of the devil. And when he had fasted forty days and forty nights, he was afterward an hungered" (Matt. 4:1-2).__* This man as God manifested in the flesh, realized that if He was going to fight the Devil He could not fight by just being a good Christian, He had to put on power. Fasting will put you in place where you will be able to quench every fiery dart of the Devil. Jesus was tempted as we have been tempted. Although there were times His flesh also wanted to give in, but He did not obey His flesh. In Matthew 26, Jesus said, *__" 'My soul is exceeding sorrowful, even unto death, tarry ye here and watch with me.' And he went a little further, and fell on his face, and prayed, saying, 'O my Father, if it be possible, let this cup pass from me; nevertheless not as I will, but thou wilt'… He went away again the second me, and prayed, saying, 'O my Father if this cup may not pass, away from me, except I drink it, thy will be done' " (Matt. 26:38-39, 42).__* Without a doubt, we can see that through His determination, He overcame the world, and He has also given us the power to overcome.

__And when the tempter came to him, he said, if thou be the Son of God, command that these stones be made bread. But he answered__ *and said, ' It is written, <u>man shall not live by bread alone, but by every word that proceedeth out of the mouth of God.</u>' Then the devil taketh him up into the holy city, and setteth him on a pinnacle of the temple. And saith unto him, 'If thou be the Son of God, cast thyself down: for it is written, <u>He shall give his angels charge concerning thee; and in their hands they shall bear thee up, lest at any time thou dash they foot against a stone.</u>' Jesus said unto him, 'It is written, again, <u>thou shall not tempt the Lord thy God.</u>' Again the devil taketh him up into an exceeding high mountain, and showeth him all the kingdoms of the world, and the glory of them. And saith unto him, 'all these will I give thee, if thou wilt fall down and worship me.' Then saith Jesus unto him, 'Get thee hence, Satan: for it is written, <u>thou shalt worship the Lord thy God, and him only shalt thou serve.</u>' Then the devil leaveth him, and, behold, angels came and ministered unto him. (Matt. 4:3-11)*

You will not be able to successfully speak the word back to the Devil unless you have power to stand. Jesus was tempted and He had to fast to get ready for spiritual warfare, what about you and I? Jesus was swayed by the spirit to follow the Devil and was tempted, but He never fell. When the Devil sends his agents to fight you, he does not send them to unknown territory; rather, he comes with that which you are familiar. After several unsuccessful attempts, the tempter was told by Jesus, "Thou shalt not tempt the Lord thy God." In other words, Jesus was letting the Devil know that He was superior to Satan and all of his foolish temptations. After the Devil realized he could not get Jesus to worship, he left Him alone. Fasting will give you immeasurable power with God to stand on His word. The law was never weak through the flesh, but man could not keep the law. Therefore, Jesus came to show us how to destroy the works of the flesh, so that we would not be weak in the flesh.

Fasting is our spiritual resource that keeps us going forward. Many people wonder why they go through so many trials, why they are financially broke, can't find a job, why marriage failing, and instead of things getting better, they getting worse. I believe any one that would humble their soul to fast and pray will always get an answer, or the situation would rid itself. The disciples of John came to Jesus, saying, ***"Why do we and the Pharisees fast oft, but thy disciples fast not? And Jesus said unto them, 'Can the children of the bride chamber mourn, as long as the bridegroom is with them? but the days will come, when the bridegroom shall be taken away and then shall they fast' " (Matt. 9:14-15).*** The bridegroom is no longer here with us in the flesh, but He is in us through spirit. The spirit needs to be renewed, as a car needs a good tune up. The Bible says, ***"Be not drunk with wine, wherein is excess; but be filled with the spirit"*** **(Eph. 5:18).** To be filled with spirit, is to be rejuvenated over and over again. Fasting keeps a Christian fired up, because it is easier for the spirit to refill a clean temple, than a temple that is filthy.

What is the True Purpose?

The church does not need to be known as a social club, or an organizational gathering place. It should not be a place where there is no power, but it should be a breaking ground for deliverance. One of the easiest ways I have found to give people understanding of their election is to teach them. ***"Moreover whom he did predestinate, them he also called: and whom he called, them he also justified: and whom he justified, them he also glorified" (Rom. 8:30)***. The responsibility of the church is to teach husbands and wives how to have successful marriages, teach children how to handle peer pressure in school and still live a holy life, and to teach believers how to live as an over comer, and to take their rightful place in the kingdom of God. Time has been far spent building churches, raising money, having banquets, and selling chicken dinners, without the demonstration of the power of God. Many pastors are going to pastors' conferences to learn how to have a large congregation, or how to start a television ministry using the vision and ideas of other church leaders. However; it does not take a seminar to receive power with God, nor to learn how to get your church to grow.

The true success of any person of God is dependent on going back to *"Kneeology 101"*. Do you want to have a victorious life? Do you desire to have a successful ministry? Do you want to witness yokes being destroyed off the lives of hurting people? Do you desire to see sinners running to the altar to be saved? Well, if the answer to any of these questions is 'yes,' fast until you hear from God, and stay in your prayer closet. I promise, you will come out with immeasurable power to cause sickness and disease to flee, and souls will seek for you, because they will know you have favor with God.

The answer to social and economic problems will not come from the White House, but it will come from the heavenly throne of God to women and men of God willing to pay the price. God always has, and always will, speak to His people, by the mouth of His prophets. The true prophet does not mind turning his dinner plate down to seek for the power of God. If a person does not fast, after they have escaped the ills of the world, they will likely return to doing those things that are works of the flesh. You may pretend that God is using you, but only you and God will know whether or not the power is real. True power brings forth revival, and revival brings total deliverance. If people are not receiving total victory over sin, sickness, diseases, bad finances, family issues, and marital problems, there is either a lack of seeking the face of God, or a lack of obedience to the word of God. Let us not make the age-old mistake, of taking holiness for a cloak. Meaning, because you cannot see your way out of a situation it means you are going through for the sake of Christ. That is the biggest lie someone can tell against Christianity. Let us tell the whole truth about what is going on, and expose it for what it is. There are a large number of ministries that do not even talk about fasting. Some have started out on the right path, in the basement of their homes crying out to

God with fasting and prayers. However, as soon as they have made a name for themselves, fasting has ceased. Fasting keeps that fiery revival burning in any ministry. Ministry planning does not mean a group of preachers, get together at the local diner, every Tuesday for lunch to discuss church politics. We have eaten enough, and if the Devil can keep preachers, eating and being gluttonous, he will sit back and laugh. Then we will have the impression that we are doing God's service because of the size of the congregation, but we will still be displeasing God.

The word of the Lord came to Joel the son of Pethuel. Hear this, ye [elders], and give ear, all ye inhabitants of the land. Hath this been in your days, or even in the days of your fathers? Tell ye your children of it, and let your children tell their children and their children another generation. That which the palmerworm hath left hath the locust eaten; and that which the locust hath left hath the cankerworm eaten; and that which the cankerworm hath left hath the caterpillar eaten. Awake, ye drunkards, and weep; and howl, all ye drinkers of wine, because of the new wine, for it is cut off from your mouth. For a nation is come up upon my land, strong, and without number, whose teeth are the teeth of a lion, and he hath the cheek teeth of a great lion. He hath laid my vine waste, and barked my fig tree: he hath made it clean bare, and cast it away; the branches thereof are made white...The meat offering and the drink offering is cut off from the house of the Lord; the priests, the Lord's ministers, mourn. The field is wasted, the land mourneth; for the corn is wasted: the new wine is dried up, the oil languisheth. Be ye ashamed, O ye husbandmen; howl,O ye vinedressers, for the wheat and for the barley; because the harvest of the field is perished. The vine is dried up, and the fig tree languisheth; the pomegranate tree, the palm tree also, and the apple tree, even all the trees of the field, are withered: because joy is withered away from the sons of men. Gird yourselves, and lament, ye priests: howl, ye ministers of the altar; come, lie all night in sackcloth, ye ministers of my God: for the meat offering and the drink offering is withholden from the house of your God. Sanctify ye a fast, call a solemn assembly, gather the elders and all the inhabitants of the land into the house of the Lord your God, and cry unto the Lord. (Joel 1:1-14)

"Blow the trumpet in Zion, sanctify a fast, call a solemn assembly: Gather the people, sanctify the congregation, assemble the elders, gather the children, and those that suck the breasts: let the bridegroom go forth of his chamber, and the bride out of her closet. Let the priests, the ministers of the Lord, weep between the porch and the altar, and let them say, Spare thy people, O Lord, and give not thine heritage to reproach, that the heathen should rule over them: wherefore should they say among the people, Where is their God?" (Joel 2:15-17)

God was attempting to bring revival back to His people, but they were going to have to work for it. Often people have a desire to be the best they can be inside and outside of ministry, but they are not willing to do what it takes to make that happen. There are three types of people in life:

1. the person who makes things happen,

2. the person who watch things happen, and

3. the person who does not know what is happening.

The Lord was telling the priests and elders that some things had gone wrong. The palmerworm, locust, cankerworm, and caterpillar were at that time having a field day with the church. The enemy has come against the vine (Jesus) and cast away the branches (the saints). The place of planting was wasted, and the new wine (the anointing) was dry. That which was supposed to produce seed was not producing, due to a lack of seeking the face of God. God spoke to Joel and told him that if revival was going to break out, the priests, the elders, and the church, including the babies, needed to seek God through fasting and prayer. Thus, the Lord was saying, 'if you want to put a muzzle on the Devil, so that he does not continue to rule you, seek Me!'

Les Brown said in his literary piece, Live Your Dreams,

"If you want a thing bad enough to go out and fight for it, to work day and night for it, to give up your time, your peace and your sleep for it... if all that you dream and scheme is about it, and life seems useless and worthless without it... if you gladly sweat for it and fret for it and plan for it and lose all your terror of the opposition for it... if you simply go after that thing you want with all your capacity, strength and sagacity, faith, hope and confidence and stern pertinacity... if neither cold, poverty, famine, nor gout, sickness nor pain, of body and brain, can keep you away from the thing that you want... if dogged and grim you beseech and beset it, with the help of God, you Will get it!"

There is nothing that God would not do for anyone that would dare to seek Him with their whole heart. Most bodybuilders use supplements in order to enhance their physique, likewise must the child of God use fasting to enhance their spiritual soul and body. Apostle Paul said: *"But I keep under my body, and bring it into subjection: lest that by any means, when I have preached to others, I myself should be a castaway" (I Cor. 9:27).* Child of God, fasting will keep the flesh in subjection to the things that are Godly. As a man needs water to live, a car needs gas to drive, a church needs people to operate it, and a flower needs sunlight to grow, so does the body need fasting, to prevent us from completely turning back to the things of our past. *"For if after they have escaped the pollutions of the world through the knowledge of the Lord and Savior Jesus Christ, they are again entangled therein, and overcome, the latter end is worse with them than the beginning. For it had been better for them not to have known the way of righteousness, than, after they have known it, to turn from the holy commandment delivered unto them." (II Pet. 2:20-21)*

Apostle. Dr. P.W. Reed, Ph.D.

Chapter - 2

Misconceptions about Fasting

The fast that the Lord has ordained will cause supernatural changes in the life of the believer, but we must understand that God's ordained fast, might not comply with the new age fast that some churches have decided to implement. Some leaders have compromised the order of God, to suit what man has decided they would accept. What God has ordained in the Old Testament for fasting, He has come to fulfill in the New Testament. Many Christians have decided that they will fast for 40 days eating one meal a day, and call it a forty-day fast. I suggest, simply eat one meal a day, for forty days, but do not call that a fast, because it is not. When Jesus fasted for forty days, he went for forty-day without eating or drinking anything. That was truly a fast.

Today we live in the microwave generation; people like things quick, fast and in a hurry. They do not want to wait until their food is completed on a gas lit stove, thus they zap it in a microwave. They say, 'child I'm hungry right now, I can't wait for that food to finish cooking on that stove. It takes too long.' In the same way Christians say, 'I don't want to wait on God for my answer, I believe I'm going to help God out, because He's taking too long to give me my answer.' Others think, 'I'm tired of waiting on a husband, I'm going to start looking for one, otherwise I will turn into an old maid.' This is the flesh speaking because it has no ability to be patient. Fasting causes the flesh to go against the grain. The flesh does not want to be controlled, but wants to be in control. Thus, it always encourages you to eat and cry out for the things it desires. Now do not misunderstand me, we all need to eat in order to live a healthy life. However, eating should be done in moderation.

There are people who fast drinking sodas, orange juice, tea, coffee, or herbal drinks. Personally I have never read in the Bible where the flesh was so comfortable fasting. When you substitute natural drinks for food, you are still being weak to the flesh by feeding it. When we fast the way that God has ordained, the flesh is denied and is forced into subjection. To put under subjection means to lock down, incarcerate or put in jail. When someone is incarcerated, he/she looses his/her civilian privileges, and becomes an inmate. In other words, they must now comply with the rules of that governing state and warden. The inmate does not eat when he desires, he does not dress the way he might desire, neither does he/she shower when they desires. They live according to the rules that have already been established. God's ordained fast is designed to take the natural privileges away from the flesh. The flesh and soul are to become uncomfortable. The person who fasts tells his flesh that he is in control; he is showing the flesh who is the boss. A boss does not comply with the demands of his or her employees; however, the workers must comply with those established by the boss or risk termination. The reason why so many people are taking their lives is that their flesh is out of control. We have been trained that if you give something up, you must replace it with something else. People nationwide believe that if something does not go in their stomach for a few days, they will die, and that is not true at all.

There are people who view fasting as not eating for a few hours. That is not the fast that God has ordained either. If someone sees himself or herself getting out of control eating, not eating for a few hours is good. Today, people are eating, just to eat. There are people that wake up in the middle of the night, and they say, 'oh, I'm just getting a midnight snack.' Yet they go every night or too often. These people have a tendency to run to the refrigerator as if it is a rest room, to let the draught go free. Everywhere you go you see people eating in their cars, on the highway, eating at the bus stop, and in stores. Very simply put, eating has gotten out of hand and has become gluttonous. Why is it that the minute someone wants to discuss business, the first place he thinks of to close a deal, is the restaurant? Or when a young man wants to come off as a gentleman, and wants to portray a certain image to his newly found friend, he invites her to dinner?

The Way It Is

Fasting was never designed to be a horn of your spirituality. It is not like shouting 'I QUIT' throughout the office so everyone can hear how bold you are. When you fast, it is a secret between you and God. Fasting causes the flesh to cry out, because it has been put in jail. Since the flesh is no longer being pampered, it will cry out. You will get migraine headaches, stomach growls and even weak legs. Outwardly, when people notice you not eating, they will offer to pamper your flesh by asking you out to lunch, whether or not they like you.

People will notice you because the physical results of fasting will become evident to those around you. I can remember when I gave my life to the Lord, how my pastor was going to baptize everyone in the church who had given their life to God. He stood before the church and declared, "before I baptize you all, I want everyone that claims Jesus Christ as their Savior to start a seven day fast." My heart fell to my knees, although I knew nothing about fasting. I soon learned that during this fast I could not have anything to eat or drink, except little sips of spring water. All I could think about was the fact that I was a bodybuilder, and I was going to lose more weight than I wanted to lose.

Nonetheless, my pastor prepared us for the fast first by teaching us what the word of God stated in reference to fasting and prayer. Immediately after he conducted the teachings on fasting I was very curious about doing it. Yet, how was I to go seven days without eating? I thought he was out of his mind. I can never forget the words that came out of my mouth, which were, "this man must be tripping." I prepared to start the fast, but before I did, I asked him, whether I would die going on this fast. He replied, "Son you'll be all right." At the time, I was working for a supermarket in New Orleans, LA. pulling filled milk carts off tractor trailers. That was the longest seven days of my life. The days got longer, and the nights did not seem like they were ever going to end. When I started my fast, I woke up and my stomach was growling, but I did not give in to it. The second day my head started to hurt, but I did not give in to that either, because in my preparation, I learned that these things could happen on the fast. On this fast, I sought the Lord for my own personal deliverance from things the Devil thought he had me bound to. I studied my Bible every chance I got, and went in the back of the supermarket on my lunch break to pray.

While I was at a Wednesday Evening Bible Study I received strength through the word of God. In fact, I suddenly realized I was on my way. My pastor, then asked everyone who was fasting to stay for a shut in for the rest of the week, which I did. Thursday morning, I went back to work fully revived. I was ready for anything Satan would send my way. I have always lost weight rapidly, thus by the forth day I had lost over twelve pounds. I was completely focused on killing out my flesh, and tearing down that terrible temper I had. I wanted to see if this "fasting stuff" would really work for me.

After leaving work, I went straight back to the church for the shut in. The power of God began to move in our church, as I had never experienced in a church before. I began to fully understand what Pentecost was like. People, who needed miracles or salvation, healing and deliverance, were coming to our church. I witnessed the blind receive their sight, the lame walk, and cancer dry up, as if it never existed. The ministry and I were experiencing it. By the time the fast was over, I had lost 22 lbs., but I was not worried about my weight, or continuing to pursue my dream of becoming a professional bodybuilder. After that seven day fast, my life began to change and the Lord made a real man of God out of me. I was single and at the time, I was taught that if you desire not to just to be another preacher, seek for the power of God through fasting. We increased the number of days we would fast from seven to ten, then ten to fourteen, and I have fasted 21 days without food or water.

I soon realized that fasting was the key to having yokes of bondage destroyed upon a person's life, no matter what the bondage was. The Lord is truly willing and able to set the captive free.

Revival Comes Through Fasting

What is the fast the Lord has ordained? Isaiah explained it as so,

Wherefore have we fasted, say they, and thou seest not? Wherefore have we afflicted our soul, and thou takest no knowledge? Behold, in the day of your fast ye find pleasure, and exact all your labors. Behold, ye fast for strife and debate, and to smite with the fist of wickedness: ye shall not fast as ye do this day, to make your voice to be heard on high. Is it such a fast that I have chosen? a day for a man to afflict his soul? Is it to bow down his head as a bulrush, and to spread sackcloth and ashes under him? Wilt thou call this a fast, and an acceptable day to the Lord? Is not this the fast that I have chosen? to loose the bands of wickedness, to let the oppressed go free, and that ye break every yoke? Is it not to deal thy bread to the hungry, and that thou bring the poor that are cast out to thy house?

when thou seest the naked, that thou cover him; and that thou hide not thyself from thine own flesh? Then shall thy light break forth as the morning, and thine health shall spring forth speedily: and thy righteousness shall go before thee; and the glory of the Lord shall be thy rereward. Then shalt thou call, and the Lord shall answer; thou shall cry, and he shall say. Here I am (Is. 58:3-8)

The Lord said, people sought Him daily and they took delight in approaching Him for answers nor did they forsake His ordinances. However, there was still something missing from the way they sought God. When we come to God, we must go beyond our natural limitations. If we want to hear from God, we have to put ourselves in a place, to be in His presence. The house of Jacob sought God, but not with the proper attitude. They complained to God that they have been fasting and He was not paying them any attention. In other words, God you are not moving for us when we think you ought to! You are not even taking notice of what we are doing. The Lord, however, answered and told them, the reason they were not getting any answers was because:

- ✞ They were exploiting their fasts through normal pleasures. Today people find pleasures, or exploit our fast by still having fun, watching TV, talking on the phone, laughing and playing games, going to the shopping centers. The Lord was letting the house of Israel know, that they had not changed from their normal ways, while they were fasting.

- ✞ They were fasting with the wrong motivations in mind: for strife, debate, and to smite with the fist of wickedness (making trouble being messy). When you fast with these motives you cause confusion, you are angry and you are fighting. Child of God, when you fast you should to get by yourself, if at all possible, and try to avoid communication and distractions as much as possible. The Devil knows that if he can get you around certain people, places, and things, he can use any of these tools to make you break your fast. It may not even be your desire to argue, but here comes someone sent as an agent of the Devil, to cause you to become negatively stirred up. You do not fast to become a skilled fighter. If you should find that you are being suckered into arguing, it means you have broken your fast, because fighting is not what God has intended to occur while you fast.

✝ They aimed to make their voice heard on high by fasting to be seen, or to become popular. God does not bless His children for them to become high and lifted up. The Bible says, **"God resisteth the proud, but giveth grace unto the humble "(James 4:6)**. Humility moves the heart of God. **"For whomsoever exalteth himself shall be abased: and he that humbleth himself shall be exalted" (Lk. 14:11).** God's children do not need to fast to be seen nor heard; when He raises you up, the whole world will know. When you try to fit in with the popular crowd, they will get tired of you, but the Lord will never leave you, nor forsake you.

The Lord told His people the fast that He has chosen is a day for a man to afflict his soul. The fast is designed to make the inner man (soul) cry or starve. The flesh will respond that it does not agree with this fast. Nonetheless, if a fast is a day for a man to afflict his soul, it should be done for a minimum of 24 hours. Thus, whatever time you start your fast, you should finish the next day, but do not try to come off an hour early. If you do this, you would have broken your fast, showing that you were concentrating more on time than on spiritual results. Do not pay attention to time, because if you do, your spirit will begin to cry out for food and command you to break your fast.

God also teaches us that it is not proper to fast walking around with your head hanging like a bulrush or dejectedly. The fast the Lord has chosen will loose wickedness, undo heavy burdens, remove oppression, and destroy every yoke of bondage. Thus, we should be loosed of heaviness in our demeanor. God's ordained fast was also designed to prove your sincerity. The person who fasts shows God that he is serious about his faith and prayers. When it is done correctly, you or the person for which the fast was designated, will be the recipient of the blessing. In addition, fasting will loose the heavy burdens of worrying, and anxiety. Every yoke of bondage upon your life, or the person that you may fast for, will be destroyed.

Fasting causes us to see those areas of our life, which we were not sensitive to before. It teaches that husband, who found it hard to show his wife he loves her, how to love properly. Fasting will teach a mean, arrogant person how to be sweet. You may have not been interested in feeding the hungry, but you will do it now. Fasting will cause you to show love immeasurably. The Bible asks, **"whoso hateth this world's good, and seeth his brother have need, and shutteth up his bowels of compassion from him, how dwelleth the love of God in him?" (I John 3:17)** However, when you fast people will see you walking down the street and know for a fact that you are a blessed man or woman of God. Your health will improve immediately, and when you call on God, and He will answer.

If your attention is not correctly guided by the spirit of God, distractions will cause you to break your fast. I am reminded of a man of God, who came out of Judah by the word of the Lord. God had sent him down to Bethel and when he had gotten there, he saw the King Jeroboam standing by the altar burning incense. Now this man of God started off wonderfully, as he cried against the altar and spoke the word of God. He told Jeroboam that the altar would be torn, and the ashes would be poured upon it. Therefore, this man of God knew that God was speaking to him. King Jeroboam was so angry at what he heard, that he took his hand to grab the man, but his hand dried up. The king cried unto the prophet and asked him to call upon God for him, so that his hand would be restored. The prophet prayed to God and the king's hand was indeed, restored to normal. The king began to fear God and became so excited that he invited this prophet to come and have dinner with him at the palace. The man of God was focused, however, on what God told him. The Lord commanded the man of God to fast (no bread nor water) and not to return the same way that he came to the city. The prophet truly was standing strong, and he appeared to be completely focused on what God had spoken to him.

There lived in Bethel an old prophet, whose sons came and told him about this prophet who had entered their city as well as what was going on, including the miracles they had seen wrought. Their father said, show me where this man is, that came out of Judah. The old prophet went galloping on a donkey and found the man of God sitting under an oak tree. The old prophet asked him if he was the man of God from Judah to which he responded yes.

The old prophet was sent to test this man of God, just as the Devil comes to test any person that would go on a fast. Do not make the mistake of thinking that when you fast, rose petals will be strewn at your feet. If you do, you will soon be disappointed because Satan knows that there is much power to be gained by fasting, besides unlimited access to God. Thus, he will do whatever is in his power to get you to break your fast.

The old prophet, told the prophet who came from Judah, to come and go home with him. The prophet from Judah boldly spoke God's commandments to the old prophet from Bethel, thus declining his offer. By making a stand, this prophet from Judah was saying, 'I am insulted that you would even make such a suggestion.' The prophet from Bethel, however, did not stop there, as he said, 'I am a prophet just like you are and an angel spoke to me and said to bring you back home with me, and you may eat bread and drink water.'

Each person must have his or her own personal relationship with God. It does not matter if they are being pastored, they must hear from God themselves. I am not trying to negate the role of pastors (I myself am a pastor). A pastor will minister to your spiritual needs and will also advise you. However, there are certain answers you need to get directly from God. While you are pursuing your own personal answers during your fast, all kinds of things will happen, including people being used as instruments of Satan without even knowing it. His ultimate goal will be to get you to break your fast, because he does not want you to receive your blessing. Thus, do not be fooled or weak.

God does not tempt, neither can He be tempted with evil. God will, however, permit your adversary to tempt you. If you are not tested, you will never truly know what you possess. Tests come to try your level of obedience, your integrity, and your character. The prophet from Judah appeared to be a man of integrity; however, we would not have known if he truly was unless he had been tested. I define character as the way people see you, but integrity as that which you really are in the absence of others.

Therefore, the prophet from Judah gave in and went back to the home of the old prophet, where he ate and drank. As they were eating, the word of God for the prophet from Judah came to the old prophet saying, ***"forasmuch as you have disobeyed the mouth of the Lord, and have not kept the commandment of the Lord, but went back and ate bread and drunk water, when I God told you what to do and what you should not do. Your carcass shall not lie with your fathers" (I Kings 13)***. After the prophet from Judah left the old prophet's house, a lion was waiting to destroy him.

All of the people of the city saw this man's body lying in the street and said, ***"is not this the man of God, who disobeyed God" (I Kings 13)***. It is a sin to break a fast, so if you are not completely serious about it and have not properly prepared yourself for it, do not do it. After examining this story, I understand fully, why Paul spoke that he was ***"persuaded that neither death, nor life, nor angel, nor principalities, nor powers, nor things present, nor things to come, nor height nor***

depth, nor any other creature, shall be able to separate us from the love God, which is in Christ Jesus our Lord." (Rom. 8:38-39)

Just looking at the scripture as it related to the prophet that broke his fast for a piece of bread and a drink of water shows us that nothing is worth it. The old prophet told the prophet from Judah that an angel spoke to him, but God never spoke this to him. In other words, if God did not confirm what someone else says, and the Lord has already shown you what to do, be obedient to God, and not to the word of an angel or a man. The Lord knows how to alter His own words; He does not need someone else to do it for Him. That is why Paul said he would not even let an angel separate him from the love of God. Remember, Lucifer himself was an angel, but he was dispelled from heaven due to his disobedience. Thus be careful of who you listen to.

God's ordained fast is not to be taken lightly. If God has ordained a fast, it means He has ordered it. When God has ordered something, no devil in hell nor your personal desire will tamper with God's plan. If you tell someone that God has ordained for you to fast, you are saying God has given you the right, because He has commanded it. When God commands, He expects the job to be done. If the Lord has commanded you to fast, He knows that you need to fast, because He wants to give you a spiritual breakthrough. It could be compared to a person having a calling from God on their life to preach the gospel, and it seems like everywhere they go, someone else is confirming their calling, but they reject it. That person may run, but they will not be able to hide from God. Whatever He has to do to get your attention, He will do. As George Bush, Jr. said, "by any means necessary."

The proper way to go on God's ordained fast was the way the old Pentecostals taught. It was done in a way, which would cause the Devil's knees to shake. We did not eat or drink anything, but spring water, even if it was a short fast, for instance three or five days. If the days extended beyond five days and we were going to preach, teach or go to our jobs, we would only sip spring water. We fully relied on the strength of the Lord and the prayers of the saints. Nevertheless, there are certain things you should do, while you are fasting. You should still brush your teeth, comb your hair, look and appear lively, and have a great time seeking the face of God. In other words, do not neglect your personal hygiene. Should the Lord tell someone to fast, He will order the number of days, because after all, the fast would not be controlled by him, but by God. I have not read in the Bible, where men and women of God who truly sought the face of God were eating and drinking. If that were at all the case, it would not be called a fast.

Do you want to truly be a man or woman of God with power, to cast out devils, take on serpents (going right where Satan's territory is), to heal the sick and to raise the dead? If that is what you really want, it is going to take more than just being a believer. You are going to have to show God that you are serious. I do not want you to misunderstand me. I know that the Bible says, ***"that these signs should follow them that believe; In my name they shall cast out devils; they shall speak with new tongues; They shall take up serpents and if they drink any deadly thing it shall not hurt them, they shall lay hands on the sick, and they shall recover" (Mk. 16 :17-18).*** However, let us not be ignorant of the fact that not everyone who is saved casts out devils, even if they have the Holy Ghost. All true believers that have been baptized in the Holy Ghost will speak with other tongues, however, not all believers will have power to raise the dead. The manifestation of this kind of power comes through fasting and prayer.

Chapter - 3

Preparation

Preparation for a fast is vitally important due to the extreme mental and spiritual fight that some might have. If the saint of God does not prepare properly, he/she will suffer the loss of their fast. Thus, it is important to know that several things will occur, which you must be ready for, such as:

1. Temptation to eat.
2. Excessive talking, when you should be studying to be quiet. (I Thess. 4:11)
3. Losing your spiritual reward, because you are impatient; you are more concerned about how soon the fast will be over.
4. Vessels of Satan are used to draw you away through shopping where your legs will start getting weak and then you feel forced to eat, to satisfy your flesh.
5. People offering to feed you, although they never had before.
6. Intimacy with your spouse during the fast (this is not permitted).
7. Arguing with children, relatives, or those in your surroundings.
8. Loss of patience, quietness, withdrawal

There are many other forms of temptations that will come to tempt you from completing your fast. If the Devil tried to make Jesus break His fast, who are you? Do not ever believe for one moment that you are Mr. or Mrs. Invincible, and that you cannot break a fast, because if you are not completely sold out for the consecration you will not be successful.

Getting Your Heart and Mind Right

If you have determined within yourself that it is time for you to fast for what ever reason, or God has commanded you to fast, the first thing you must do is to develop a sense of commitment. In other words, mentally you will make a covenant between yourself and God that you will be dedicated to worship in the form of your fast. Paul said, ***"I beseech you therefore, brethren, by the mercies of God, that ye present your bodies as a living sacrifice, holy, acceptable unto God, which is your reasonable service. And be not conformed to this world: but be ye transformed by the renewing of your mind, that ye may prove what is that good, and acceptable, and perfect, will of God" (Rom. 12:1-2).***

Paul was indicating to the saints of God at Rome that to see a change take place in their lives and in the lives of others, proper fasting, was in order. In this context, the fast is our sacrifice to God. Thus, anyone who is going to fast must make sure that the sacrifice is holy. The Lord has never accepted a sacrifice that was filthy. Holiness first begins in the heart. If my heart has not changed, my life will not change either. Paul wrote to the saints that if they wanted to sacrifice, they would have do it in a way that God would honor it, so that the sacrifice would not be in vain.

While fasting, you cannot focus on your job, running around buying groceries, or going to the shopping malls. That is conforming to the world. Your mind must be transformed first, that you may be able to prove the sincerity of your reasonable service.

Fasting Preparation

1. Determine within yourself that you do not have a problem pushing the dinner plate aside.
2. While mentally preparing for your fast, begin to minimize your food intake.
3. Then wash your thoughts of any unclean things that can defile your spiritual man. You do not want to start a fast with unclean thoughts.
4. If there are any unresolved issues, settle them correctly before you start your fast. Often people want to be used of God, but they do not want to do the simple things like making sure their heart is right, before they go on a consecration. If you feel as though you do not like someone, do not start a fast on top of your dislike, because that spirit will become more revived at the conclusion of your fast. We cannot skip over our brother or sister when things are not in order and just talk to God in prayer. Go to your brother of sister first, then ask God to forgive you for the way you felt.
5. Anoint your head with oil- get your mind right
6. Provided you have never fast before stop eating heavy foods and start eating fruits, vegetables, and unsweetened juices

But I say unto you, that whosoever is angry with his brother without a cause shall be in danger of the judgment: and whosoever shall say… Thou fool, shall be in danger of hell fire. Therefore if thou bring thy gift to the altar, and there rememberest that thy brother hath ought against thee; Leave there thy gift before the altar, and go

thy way: first be reconciled to thy brother, and then come and offer thy gift. (Matt. 5:22-24)

Don't you dare be foolish enough to fast, preach, teach, sing, or testify on top of knowing there are issues that must be put in order! God respects a person who is honest. When you have made it right with whomever you need to, pick your gift up and go on with the Lord. If John or Sally desires to stay upset with you, pray for him/her, and go on with the Lord, but do not allow yourself to be stuck in that rut of unforgiveness.

Get Prayed Up!

Jesus told the disciples that men ought always to pray and not faint (Luke 18:1). If you pray you will not faint, and if you do not pray you will faint. Is it possible that you can always pray or is that just a figure of speech? I believe with all of my heart that men can always pray and they do not have to faint. Let us first understand that prayer is defined as: Asking for earnestly; to worship God; communion with God; supplication, or devotion.

Prayer is the link between God and man. When man prays, he proves to God that he desires to be in communion with Him. There are things I can pray for with my understanding, such as praying for my enemies, and for myself, that I do not reciprocate evil for evil, but overcome evil with my good. It can be very difficult to pray for someone who spitefully uses you, and persecutes you. This difficulty can be overcome, however, if we pray always. When we are consistently in prayer, we revive the God consciousness in us. Prayer causes us to change when we do not feel there are areas in our lives that need to be changed. As we begin to prepare for the fast and become prayed up, we are asking God to show us how frail we are. In doing so, we will soon realize these frailties. Sally will find that she is not as sweet as she thought, and Jim will see how selfish he has been in his relationship.

How can I pray when I am on my job or transacting business? There is such as prayer called the secret prayer, which is between you and God. In this prayer, no one knows that you are praying. I can stand right in the midst of a tumultuous situation, and at the same time in my spirit and mind, I am binding the Devil, yet no one hears me, but the Lord. He responds by ceasing every bad situation around me without me even having to open my mouth. I may have secretly spoken this prayer in my heart, but God honored it openly. There may be times, when you are not in position to pray openly. All you have to do is think the prayer in your mind, and God will move just as greatly as if the prayer had been spoken. I have been in positions where the Devil has tried to attack me in my sleep, and it was as though he tried to muzzle my mouth. However, I moaned "Jesus," and the Devil had to flee. While you are on your job in the midst of unbelievers, all you have to do is smile and pray with your inner man. As a result God will began to move on your behalf. Many may not know, but waking up in the morning with a smile on your face thanking God for another day, is a form of devotional prayer. It is called the prayer of thanksgiving. I have seen true women of God, vacuuming the floor or mopping the church with tears rolling down their faces, because they are thankful that God has given them an opportunity to work for Him. Those tears of joy are a form of worship.

Therefore, before I begin a fast, I prepare my temple. The Bible says, **"watch and pray that ye enter not into temptation" (Matt. 26:41)**. Jesus rose up very early in the morning to pray, so if we are going to be like Him, we must do what He did. There is no cut and dried formula to power. Watching and praying here refers to being prayerful but also alert and sensitive to your surroundings. Thus, when the tempter comes during your fast, you will now be ready for him.

And when thou prayest, thou shalt not be as the hypocrites are: for they love to pray standing in the synagogues and in the corners of the streets, that they may be seen of men. Verily I say unto you,

They have their reward. But thou, when thou prayest, enter into thy closet, and when thou hast shut thy door, pray to the Father which is in secret, and thy Father which seeth in secret shall reward thee openly. But when ye pray, use not vain repetitions, as the heathen do: for they think that they shall be heard for their much speaking. Be not ye therefore like unto them: for your Father knoweth what things ye have need of, before ye ask him. (Matt. 6:5-8)

There were some people, including religious leaders, who wanted to be seen as "really spiritual," and worshipped publicly using their prayer to get attention. Jesus did not look upon them as being "deep," but rather ignorant and self-righteousness. Jesus taught that the essence of prayer was not public notoriety but private communication with God. There are times believers will be forced to pray in a public setting, but to only pray where others will see you is an indication of your falseness. Your focus is obviously not God, but people. The point here is that praying loudly in church to be seen will not move the hand of God any faster than the person quietly praying at the bus stop. Let us note that fasting is done in secret, and there are times when your prayer should also be done in your secret closet. This type of prayer will get you ready for any fast. You do not have to repeatedly utter the same words while you are pray. After you get a break through on that petition, move on!

Because of your earnest prayers and sacrifices, you will earn favor with God. Due to this favor with God, you will be able to think things into existence through prayer. You may never open your mouth, but God knows the desire of your heart, and He will choose to bless you with it. The Lord told Isaiah, ***"And it shall come to pass that before they call, I will answer; and while they are yet speaking I will hear." (Isaiah 65:24).***

During your prayer time before you start your fast, remember to ask God to keep you from falling into temptations, distractions or anything that might hinder you from completing your fast and He will keep you.

Study To Be Approved

We would agree that all those who profess Christianity should have a pastor, to teach them the word of God. However, it is just as important for all Christians to seek God through the scriptures for themselves. The Bible says, **"Search the scriptures; for in them ye think ye have eternal life: and they are they which testify of me" (John 5:39).** There is no way you can witness about someone you do not know. How can we testify of a Savior whom we know nothing of? In order to communicate salvation to someone who is lost, you must first develop a personal relationship with the Lord for yourself.

It is impossible to develop a relationship with God, if you do not know what the word of the Lord says. I will give you an example of a similar, so-called relationship. Mr. Jones was the owner of the ABC Company. He came to work diligently and when his employees saw him coming in, they regarded him with the highest degree of respect. Every morning Johnny, one of Mr. Jones's employees, was there to open the door for Mr. Jones as he briskly walked through the door. Johnny greeted Mr. Jones each day, and Mr. Jones would eloquently respond back, with a warm smile or an elated hello! This, however, was as far as the conversation usually went. Johnny, however, got excited, and would tell his family at home about how great Mr. Jones was and how wonderfully Mr. Jones treated him.

During the holidays, Mr. Jones threw a Christmas party at the Ritz Carleton Hotel, for all his important friends His board of directors came, along with the vice presidents, their wives, and his supervisors. All of the attendees knew Mr. Jones well, on a first name basis, and so they were not afraid to tell Harry about how wonderful the party was and how glad they were to have been invited.

Meanwhile, Johnny was sitting at home wondering why he was not invited. Resolved to go thinking that maybe Mr. Jones forgot to send him an invitation, he rushed to get dressed then made his way to the beautiful Ritz Carleton Hotel. At the front desk he asked the clerk, "where is the company party, for the ABC Company?" and the clerk directed him to the fifth floor. Johnny arrived and opened the door to the ballroom, excited to be there. To his dismay, the door person asked, "Where is your invitation?" Johnny replied, "I have none." However, Johnny asked the door person, to call Mr. Jones, to straighten out the problem.

When Mr. Jones came to the door, to find out what the problem was Johnny asked him why he had not received his invitation to the party. Mr. Jones responded that he never knew Johnny. Johnny had never gotten to know Mr. Jones. He said, 'all I can remember is that you open the door for me everyday, but I didn't know you were one of my employees, I thought you were just being nice, young man. Now, can you please leave!' Needless to say, Johnny walked away feeling very sad and dejected, saying, I thought I knew him!

You do not know the Lord just because you've heard someone preach about Him, because you have repented of your sins, or because you go to church every Sunday and occasionally to a Tuesday Evening Bible study. You must pursue your own relationship with Him to be invited into His heavenly kingdom. Fasting and prayer will help to establish this relationship. Searching the scriptures before a fast will give you food that will be stored up in your spiritual man, so that when the adversary comes, you will have something within you to fight him. Examining the scriptures will also show you what it means to be in covenant with God, why fasting is important, the many miracles Jesus wrought, and how they are still valid today. You will also learn of all of God's covenant blessings, which He bestows upon the children of light. There may be times when you are waiting on God for an answer, that you pick up the word of God, begin to read, and suddenly, the Lord speaks to you through His word. As Isaiah articulated, ***"To the law and to the testimony: if they speak not according to this word, it is because there is no light in them"(Isaiah 8:20)***. Because you have sought the Lord for yourself, whenever you hear something contrary to the scriptures, whether via prophesy or preaching of the gospel, you will know not to receive it. Therefore, we must search the scriptures for deliverance, answers, knowledge and truth.

"Study to shew thyself approved unto God, a workman that needeth not to be ashamed, rightly dividing the word of truth. But shone profane and vain babblings: for they will increase unto more ungodliness." (2 Tim. 2:15-16)

If we study the word of God, we will not have to error or be made fools of. Our belief in the lord Jesus Christ will be validated by what we know. Thus, it is very important to develop good study habits before you start your fast, because, while you are fasting it will make it much easier to be disciplined. There will be manifold mysteries that will be revealed to you, and you will began to understand scriptures that you could not understand prior to the fast. As you prepare yourself through good study habits, the right spirit, and by making all things right with any persons you need to, you will now be getting spiritually ready for your fast.

Clean It Up!

Making sure your body is thoroughly clean inside and out, is very important during the fast as well. You should always eat your last meal early enough so that your body can digest its food properly. Take a laxative like a magnesium citrate about an hour after eating your last meal. Use products such as milk, bananas, or ex-lax to help move your bowels. If your body does not completely rid itself of the food, you will feel it throughout your fast. You will suffer nausea, and your stomach will feel as though it constantly has gas in it. As a result, this will cause your stomach size to take a much longer time to shrink. If you take these laxatives, however, your body should feel completely empty in the morning when you awake.

As you wake up to face your day of fasting, do not make the mistake of thinking you are not supposed to brush your teeth or use a mouth wash, for that is not true. If you've been taught not to brush your teeth, someone has lied to you. You should brush your teeth as normal. It is also okay to bring a mouthwash to work with you. It is very important to remember that you should not talk directly into a person's face. Do not give yourself a bad name because of bad breath. Stand a minimum of two feet away from the person with whom you are holding a conversation.

Also, comb your hair, and as look as well as you can. As they prepare for their fast, some people pick up a lazy spirit and suddenly do not want to comb their hair. They decide, 'I'll just go to the beauty shop and get braids in my hair, so I won't have to do it myself.' Stop being lazy! Remember you do not have to turn into a Raggedy Ann Doll. You can brush your teeth, use mouthwash to kill the germs, comb your hair, and look presentable. The point is, you are a Christian, and you present yourself as one at all times.

Wear moderately bright clothes, because the clothes you wear speak quite a bit about how you feel and can influence the way you feel as well. Clothes play a vital part in a person's every day life. Picking out the right clothes, especially while preparing for a fast, will help you to make it through the day. Dull colored clothing like brown, gray or black, will make you feel gloomier than you need to feel. The brighter you dress, however, is the happier you will feel and act!

Keep the Pep in Your Step

Many people lose their spiritual or natural rewards of fasting because they try to look really 'deep' or 'spiritual' while they are fasting. They desire someone to come up to them and ask if they are fasting. Thus, they walk around looking sick and extremely pitiful, as if they want someone to do their job of fasting for them. If you desire to lose your reward, then walk around like a zombie, but don't allow everyone else to become affected by how you are feeling at that moment.

Mary starts to lose weight and it is noticeable. Someone says, "girl, you are looking so good losing all that weight, what have you been doing?" And Mary replies, "Girl, I've been fasting!" Let me tell you two things,

- ✞ do not go around telling everyone that you are fasting, and
- ✞ you do not go on a fast to lose weight. Weight loss is just one of the many things that will happen as a result of fasting.

After a fast, however, it is good to work out because while you fast you are not losing fat you are losing muscle. At one time, I was a bodybuilder, and I happen to realize that I was losing weight extremely fast; I thought that was great, I could lose weight and become closer to God at the same time. Bodybuilders do not body build to lose muscle; they do it to gain muscle. What I did not know at the time, however, was that I was either going to continue to body build or become sold out to the kingdom of God. I chose the Lord as my Savior as opposed to becoming a fulltime bodybuilder. I started fasting often and I continued to lose weight, but I had become stronger spiritually. My ministry started flourishing, and my flesh began to become submissive to God. I had now come into a relationship with Him.

Returning to my original point, realize that fasting should not be publicized. If a church fasts together, the knowledge of that fast should be kept between that ministry and its members, not their unsaved family members or friends. Also, please, if you are going to fast and are married, tell your spouse so that they will understand why you are sleeping in the den or living room!

"Moreover when ye fast, be not, as the hypocrites, of a sad countenance: for they disfigure their faces, that they may appear unto men to fast. Verily I say unto you, they have their reward. But thou, when thou fastest, anoint thine head, and wash thy face; That thou appear not unto men to fast, but unto thy Father which is in secret: and they Father which seeth in secret, shall reward thee openly." (Matt. 6:16-18)

Before you begin your fast, make sure you spend as much time as possible in prayer. A highly recommended place for prayer would be the house of God; it is the best place to get away from outside distractions. Therefore, start the morning off in prayer and if you must go to work or leave your home for an extended period of time, make sure to anoint your head with oil. In Matthew 6:16-18, Jesus referred to the ancient custom of anointing one's head before going to a feast. Anointing your head with oil will refresh you and put your mind in focus to ward off any unnecessary forces of evil that will attempt to make you break your fast. Many people break their fast because they start arguing, fighting, or because the children act up. When you anoint your head, however, you are guarding your mind.

In total, fasting should be a symbol of joy, for a happy occasion, not a sad one. Fasting teaches us self-discipline, and reminds us to appreciate God. In our behavior, it is important to remember that when we fast, we are not putting on a dramatic show to be seen. In other words, your fast should be undetected. Please do yourself a favor, and do not walk around the office with a sad face hoping that your manager will tell you to take the rest of the day off, because you look sick. Wash your face so that you can be alert and ready to take on the world. We should appear the same way we were before we started the fast, but with humility. If you are a loud individual, you should become quiet. Lastly, no matter what, keep your enthusiasm; your enthusiasm will help to keep you through the day. If your fast is done properly, you will reap the benefits of whatever you are seeking God for.

530

Apostle. Dr. P.W. Reed, Ph.D.

Chapter - 4

The True Purpose

Fasting as a Resource

How can fasting be used as a resource? This question and many more will be answered in this exciting chapter. As you roam through this chapter, you will read about testimonies of people who received miracles and deliverance through fasting. We are going to see how fasting counterattacks every trick of the Devil and gives the child of God the upper edge.

First, it is important to note that fasting is the key to releasing the power on the life of or inside of the believer. We know that signs shall follow the believer, but not every person who is a believer will operate in God's ordained power. Jesus gave His disciples power (*exousia*) (see Matt. 10:1), over unclean spirits, to cast them out, and to heal all manner of sickness and disease. However, although He gave them this, they never earned the power of authority (*dunamis*). *Dunamis* is the power of the Holy Ghost, which one must seek for himself.

There is no cut and dry formula for receiving this power, other than seeking for it through fasting and prayer. It is true that a minister will preach the gospel and you may feel ten times better than you did before you went to a revival meeting or a church service, but was there a demonstration of power? Did the minister truly operate in power? Each individual must seek God for his/her own personal relationship with Him. There is nothing better than seeking God for yourself and having your own personal relationship. As a result of your fasting and your ability to seek God for yourself, as a consecrated believer, it will be much easier for you to receive what God has in store for you.

The Lord told Jeremiah: ***"I have not sent these prophets, yet they ran: I have not spoken to them, yet they prophesied. But if they had stood in my counsel, and had caused my people to hear my words, then they should have turned them from their evil way, and from the evil of their doings." (Jer. 23:21-22)***

Many people say that God has spoken to them, and that they have a word from Him. In fairness to the Lord though, many of these people are lying on Him. In essence, God told Jeremiah in the scripture above, that these prophets claimed to speak for Him, yet He had given them no message. He continued to say that if they had heard from Him, they would have spoken His words and the people would have turned from their evil ways. There are many people joining churches, but are they hearing the gospel truth that will cause them to change?

For a servant of God to equip himself with the power that Jesus had, he will not get it from a seminary. He will have to go to the School of Kneeology and the Secret Closet. True men and women of God are equipped with the ministry of reconciliation to change lives. This will not be a little 'Pebbles and Bam Bam' shout or 'Tie My Bow Tie' Christianity. The Lord's conversion must be everlasting.

Revival is not singing, dancing or entertaining a crowd of people. Revival is the resurrection of life to those who were dead. If souls are not running to altars and throwing their drugs away willingly, or miracles are not being wrought, revival has not yet come (at least not in that service). The true God ordained revival will be a memorable revival heard abroad. As a result of these revivals, saints of God will remember the day and hour they were saved or set free. Satan's desire is to make the church look foolish. If he can get men and women to stop seeking God because they have gotten what some folks call "big time," he will have them thinking they have it 'going on.' Then when they least expect it, he will cause them to be brought to an open shame. This shame may even take place at a revival service. Try going into a revival meeting, when you have not sought God through fasting and prayer; you may not admit it, but you will probably be in your flesh.

Due to the fact that man was born with the nature of his parents, a sinful nature, there is no way possible for him to effectively preach the gospel or prophesy the word of the Lord, if he is not in tune to God. Thus, we all must first be delivered from that old sin nature wherein we were born, because we were born in sin and shaped in iniquity. Fasting will be the resource you need to fight the Devil and your sin nature.

The Devil is shaking in his boots every time he knows a child of God is fasting. Why do you think he sends spirits of distraction when a person dares to fast. Satan does not want you to have the power of God in your life.

Jesus…until the day in which he was taken up, after that he through the Holy Ghost had given commandments unto the apostles whom he had chosen: To whom also he showed himself alive after his passion by many infallible proofs, being seen of them forty days, and speaking of the things pertaining to the kingdom of God: And being assembled together with them, commanded them that they should not depart from Jerusalem, but wait for the promise of the Father which saith he, 'ye have heard of me…But ye shall receive power, after that the Holy Ghost is come upon you: and ye shall be witnesses unto me both in Jerusalem, and in all Judaea, and in Samaria, and unto the uttermost part of the earth.' (Acts 1:1-4, 8)

When Jesus told His disciples to seek for the Holy Ghost and power, they never waited. They went straight to work and started seeking God. They realized the only way that they could possibly come to know Him and the power of His resurrection, was to fast and pray. The apostles along with Mary, Jesus's mother, sought for the indwelling of the Holy Ghost. Because they meant business and were serious, the Holy Ghost fell on them on the day of Pentecost. The point here is that the recipients in the Upper Room had a mind to seek God for the power Jesus promised to send back to them. The apostles never put their jobs or any other responsibilities before God. They sought God with their whole heart, and that is why they were used by Him.

I do not fully understand how some Christians can claim to have the Holy Ghost, but there is no demonstration. When the Holy Ghost comes, there is a certain degree of power that you will possess. We would all agree that the apostles had power to raise the dead, heal the sick and give sight to the blind. Yet, today there are millions of persons professing to have the Holy Ghost, but they do not possess power. Some do not have power to live holy; to stop lying, committing adultery, and fornicating; or to become a Christian of integrity. Nevertheless, they still say they have the Holy Ghost. Someone is lying!

If we seek for the Holy Ghost that the apostles had, we would cast out devils and heal the sick, instead of sending them down to the city hospital. We would also be able to take the hand of people in wheelchairs and cause paralysis to leave their bodies, then the healed people would praise God for their healing. Every miracle that Jesus wrought was so that the Father could be glorified. Remember that the Holy Ghost, is God's spirit and if we have Him inside of us, He manifests Himself through power. The problem is that there are few who will pay a price to receive all that God has in store for their lives.

Thus, are we living in a world in which not all Christians have the true Holy Ghost? Yes! When I refer to the true Holy Ghost, I am indicating that there are Christians who have blatantly lied and said they have it, when in fact they do not. If indeed, they had God's spirit in them they would have a life to back up their claims.

"And we are his witnesses of these things, and so is also the Holy Ghost, whom God hath given to them that obey him"(Acts 5:32).

The Holy Ghost is given to those who have made up their minds that they will make every attempt to be obedient to God. The Holy Ghost is God's precious treasure that He desires to place in all believers, but if you have not received it, it is not because it is so hard to get, but maybe you have not sought it with your whole heart. Going on a fast will help you to identify what is keeping you from receiving the Holy Ghost. Fasting will reveal your sins, dislikes, nonconformities and disobedient ways. You cannot receive Godly authority until you put yourself in position. Fasting will be that resource to help you to become honest with yourself, and honesty will bring results.

"Verily, verily, I say unto you, He that believeth on me, the works that I do shall he do also; and greater works than these shall he do; because I go unto my Father. And whatsoever ye shall ask in my name, that will I do, that the Father may be glorified in the Son. If ye shall ask any thing in my name, I will do it" (John 14:12-14).

Peter and John were going into the temple at the hour of prayer, as always, when suddenly a certain man (above forty years old), was brought before them seeking for money. This man was born lame and was alone, so he learned how to be a panhandler to support himself. All of the people who knew this man felt sorry enough for him to take turns in laying him at the gate. Yet, they never told the man he could do better for himself, as opposed to being a beggar. Society had this man disbelieving in God, and accepting that he was whipped. Thus, he could not do any better than he was doing.

As Peter and John were about to enter the temple, they looked at the man. Peter told the man, 'Look at us and see our example.' He began to listen to every word they were saying to appear interested since he had learned what it was to be a con artist. He was expecting to receive something from them because of his attentiveness. Peter said, 'silver and gold is not what we have, but what we have, we will give unto you. In the name of Jesus Christ, get off the ground, stop begging, and walk.' The Bible says he took the man by the hand and immediately, his feet and ankle received strength. The man stood up, started walking, and entered into the temple with them, leaping and praising God.

Now the apostles could probably have done the opposite of what the Lord had chosen for them to do, by borrowing the money from someone to give to this poor man. However, they decided not to go that way. Instead, they used the power that they had received through God's anointing. They had paid the price, thus they were able to use the power they possessed as a resource for someone else. They gave this man a life that he had never known. Now, this man could become self-reliant, and more importantly, he could become the best Christian he could ever desire to be.

> ***"The disciple is not above his master, nor the servant above his lord. It is enough for the disciple that he be as his master, and the servant as his lord. If they have called the master of the house Beelzebub, how much more shall they call them of his household?" (Matt. 10:24-25)***

We are living in a time when people do not need to hear another preacher without power. Very soon, they will begin to wonder, "why isn't my pastor operating in God's authority?" The truth is we need more people to get the job done, even if the leaders are not doing what they should. When we fast and pray the way we should there will be no deficiencies in the body of Christ. We can see this in the following personal testimonies.

Apostle. Dr. P.W. Reed, Ph.D.

A Heart of Gold

I will never forget Sister Turner; she was a lady with a heart of Gold. During the time I knew her, I was part of a ministry in which my pastor followed the A. A. Allen Ministries in Miracle Valley. He was accustomed to holding church services all night long and never seemed to get tired. Our main service was held on Saturday evenings at 8:00 p.m. until, most times, 2:00 a.m. Sunday morning. Sister Turner was one of the first members of our church from when it began, and as I can remember, she would never miss a church service. This lady was also one of my spiritual cheerleaders when I first started preaching. If no one else showed up for church to hear me preach, she would always be on that third pew smiling saying, "Preach Brother Percy!" I began to grow strong in the word of God, and I became my pastor's assistant in the ministry.

Sister Turner would catch a ride home with my wife and I, and we all became very close. She became a great inspiration to our lives, and would help us with anything we needed. Later when we had our little girl, Sister Turner would also volunteer to watch her for us, when we needed a sitter. Furthermore, she would also make chicken dinners for us that were so good, you had to take your hat off, just to slap yourself with it. Yet, she was so modest about everything. She would not hesitate to sacrifice the last bit of anything she had for anyone else, and when she did she would never tell anyone else.

This great, inspiring woman, however, took a turn for the worst as she was hospitalized. This woman, with a heart of Gold, needed a heart transplant. The church would not accept it, so we agreed to go on a fast on her behalf and held a prayer shut-in in the church. Then, my pastor went to pray for her, along with a few of us. After we prayed the prayer of faith, she told the doctors, "I don't want a heart transplant I want to go home; the Lord has healed me!" She put her clothes on and went home. The doctors told her she would probably live two days at the most.

After she left the hospital, we brought a big lazy boy chair to the church for her to sit on and be comfortable in. Physically, she had lost a considerable amount of weight and she would come to church accompanied by an oxygen tank. Yet, we still believed the Lord had healed her.

In a month, Sister Turner regained her weight and started eating whatever she desired. We witnessed this lady walk out of that lazy boy recliner, and say that she had no business being in that chair, if the Lord had healed her. She lived a full life and did not die until five years later, by natural death in her sleep. The Lord gave the woman who had a heart of gold a new heart.

I Can Have A Baby Too!

Winnie was a young lady who gave her life to God in my living room. One of the brothers in the church I pastored in New Orleans, LA., called me and said, "Pastor, I have this lady with me, she's a prostitute and is demon possessed. She is tired of men using her body and the demons of Satan began controlling her, and causing her to do things she had no control over." Thus, the brother brought Winnie to my home, and thank God I was fasting, because I could not imagine she was so bad off. For about thirty minutes, we were in prayer for this young lady, and demons started to cry out, saying they refused to leave her. I commanded them to be subject in the name of Jesus Christ and to come out of her! The demons were forced out and began to flee by the power of God. They cried out because they were no longer able to live in her body.

About a year later, Winnie married the brother who brought her to my house for prayer. She turned her life over to God, and stopped selling her body and using crack-cocaine. Yet, she always had a desire to have a baby, but the drugs had eaten up her body, and the doctors had removed her womb. She cried as she told me as well as others this story.

One day as I was preaching, the Holy Ghost spoke to me and said, He was going to permit Winnie to have a baby girl the next year as she desired. I prophesied the word of the Lord, and every one who knew she could not have a baby, thought my prophecy was off the mark. Several came to me and said, "Pastor she has no womb, how is she going to have a baby?" I told them, "well the Lord made the womb and if He spoke it, shall he not bring it to pass?" Bring it to pass, He did. Winnie had a healthy baby girl, nine months later, without any complications. Yes, God is a miracle worker.

Cigarettes Won't Bind Me

Wendell was struggling with smoking cigarettes and he wanted to quit ever so badly. He said he had given his life to the Lord some years ago and he came to church faithfully. However, every time he would come to the house of God, he would feel so convicted and afraid that I would find out that he had this situation.

One service, after I finished preaching, I discerned that he had just smoked before he came to church. I asked him, "Brother, do you really, truly want to stop smoking, and are you Godly sorry that you've done it again?" He replied, "Brother, I really want to stop and I pray that the Lord will give me the strength to do it." I asked him if he would accompany me, on a five day fast. Wendell told me, if it would help him to overcome smoking, he definitely would.

We fasted without eating or drinking anything. The power of God was upon us both, as we believed God for his miracle. Personally, I had been fasting almost every week at that time, and I did not want to fast just to say I was fasting with someone else. Therefore, I asked God to give him a miracle and take the taste for smoking away at whatever means necessary. Wendell had not smoked for a total of five days, so I knew it was because we were fasting. I was still believing God for his miracle even after the fast was completed.

We ended the fast eating soup and crackers. He told me he felt like a new man, and did not have a desire to smoke. Several weeks had gone by, and he fell to the temptation of smoking again. This time, though, God had shown up. Wendell started choking on that cigarette and he felt as if his lungs were collapsing. Needless to say, Wendell never smoked another cigarette!

As the word of God says in I Corinthians 3:16-17, **"Know ye not that ye are the temple of God, and that the Spirit of God dwelleth in you? If any man defile the temple of God, him shall God destroy; for the temple of God is holy, which temple ye are."**

Clothed In His Right Mind

A robust gentleman escorted a young man to one of our Azusa Camp Meetings, held annually in Boston, MA., saying, "Call the man of God, and tell him this young man is demon possessed." Demons were crying out, with all sorts of vulgar language, and causing the young man to hurt himself. He rolled on the ground, saying, "I will not come out of him!" At the time, several members of our congregation had joined me on a ten-day and ten-night fast and shut in. By the time the camp meeting came, we were ready for anything the Devil might throw our way.

Several men brought the young man before the altar and I commanded the Devil to come out and let him go, in the name of Jesus! The demons became subject and the young man was lifted off the ground as he began to shout Jesus and ran around the tent. I happened to have on my best sport coat, which I had a great level of affinity for, at the time. The spirit of the Lord spoke to me, and said, "Give him your coat and teach him that he now has a new beginning." I gave him the coat without hesitation and the power of God began to fall on him again. The Lord set him free, and he was clothed in his right mind.

I Can Sleep Again

A man walked into our service one day while I was preaching, and after I preached, God led me to minister to the needs of His people through the gift of discernment and prophesy. As I was praying for several people, the spirit of the Lord led me to call this man out for prayer. As I prayed for him, God began to reveal he had sickness in his body and he could not sleep at night. After service, this man revealed to me that he had gone to several churches seeking for his healing, but for whatever reason he had not received it. We prayed the prayer of faith and God touched this man's body, as he had never experienced before. He joined the church, and set up an appointment to see me.

The day of the appointment, we sat in my office and he began to share with me the seriousness of his ailment. He told me his private body parts were always burning, and he could not sleep at night. He shared with me how at night he also felt as though there were insects crawling uncontrollably all over his body. We believed the Lord for his miracle and as we touched and agreed, the power of the Holy Ghost fell on this man. He even began speaking in other tongues as the spirit of God gave him utterance. The Lord set him free, and from that day, he started sleeping like a baby.

What can Happen if I Fast Properly?

There are many skeptics who say are fasting is not for this time. They say, "fasting is for crazy folks that are a part of a cult," "If I fast, I will die," "I'm all ready small and petite and if I fast, no one will be able to even recognize me," and "I will never fast unless I go to a city hospital, because I won't eat their food anyway!" So many people have erred due to false teachings about fasting. Thus, they are horrified to even think about doing fasting for one day, much more ten to fourteen days. Fasting, however, causes drastic changes that are unbelievable.

If ye then be risen with Christ, seek those things which are above, where Christ sitteth on the right hand of God. Set your affections on things above, not on things on the earth. For ye are dead, and your life is hid…in glory. Mortify therefore your members which are upon the earth, fornication, uncleanness, inordinate affection, evil concupiscence, and covetousness, which is idolatry: For which things' sake the wrath of God cometh on the children of disobedience: In the which ye also walked some time, when ye lived in them. But now ye also put off all these; anger, wrath, malice, blasphemy, filthy communication out of your mouth. Lie not one to another, seeing that ye have put off the old man with his deeds. And have put on the new man, which is renewed in knowledge after the image of him that created him. (Col. 3:1-10)

The key word to this great passage of scripture is "if." Many Christians feel that because they go to church, they have been risen with Christ. I am sorry to burst your bubble, but if your life has not changed, you have not been raised; you are still spiritually dead. You must crucify the old man and his ways, and there is only one way to do it! This way is not going to your pastor asking him to pray for you, reading your Bible every day, or praying often. The answer, stated in the Bible and yet still in effect for today, is fasting.

30 Spiritual Reasons Why We Should Fast

1. Fasting will make help you to get back into prayer. David said, ***"...I humbled my soul with fasting; and my prayer returned unto mine own bosom"***(Ps. 35:13). Realize that at times, your flesh will not desire to get a breakthrough, but you will have to fast to get past what the flesh desires not to do. However, because of your fasting, your heart will turn back to praying.

2. Fasting mortifies (deadens) your flesh. Remember the flesh does not die through a one day fast only. Try fasting for seven to fourteen days, and your flesh will feel as though it were dead.

3. Fasting prevents the flesh from having its own way, and commands obedience from it.

4. Fasting will cause bad habits like the following to be broken in the following ways:
   - Substance abuse users will overcome using drugs
   - The taste for tobacco and smoking will dissolve faster than nicorette gum
   - Those with lying spirits, will be anointed to tell the truth
   - The consumption of alcohol will cease and the taste for it will leave
   - Sexual impurities will stop, because the desires for it will die
   - Unclean thoughts will no longer exist

5. Fasting brings one into true holiness.

6. Fasting will bring the old, carnal nature under subjection.

7. Fasting will cause loved ones to give their lives to God.

8. If a church fasts, backsliders, new converts, drug users, homosexuals, and prominent persons in society will give their lives to God.

9. Fasting causes the natural desires of man to change in a way that he will not desire to do the things he would normally do, but rather, his desires will conform to the things of God.

10. Prayers that have not been answered- for which you have wondered why- will be answered (Matt. 17:20-21).

11. Fasting brings about spiritual and natural success.

12. Fasting will bring changes in your environment (home, job, children, and relationships with friends and spouses).

13. Individuals who felt whipped by life will begin to take the stand they were destined to take. There will be no more low-self esteem neither a lack of confidence in one's ability.

14. Fasting builds faith, character, and integrity.

15. Fasting helps our body to bear what Jesus suffered while He mortified His own flesh.

16. Fasting brings the gifts of the Spirit into manifestation.

17. Fasting destroys the works of the flesh, thereby replacing them with the fruits of the Spirit.

18. Fasting will enhance the anointing of God in any office of the ministry.

19. Fasting will give one spiritual understanding. Thus, when one hears a preacher ministering, his/her understanding will become fruitful, because there will be complete enlightenment in the word of God.

20. Fasting will open your mind to revealed knowledge from God.

21. Fasting brings one into the abundance of revelations, visions, dreams and the spirit of discernment.

22. Fasting brings spiritual empowerment and sensitivity.

23. One will become more adequately in tune to the spirit of God and its operation during and after a fast.

24. Fasting pulls down the stronghold of the Devil, and causes him to be subject.

25. Fasting rids the believer of doubt, because we receive evidence of what God can and will do through fasting.

26. Yokes that seemed to be unbreakable will be destroyed from off of your life and off of the lives of others you have fasted and prayed for.

27. Fasting causes the ministries of divine healing, miracles and laying-on of hands to come forth.

28. Fasting will enhance the abilities of any preacher who is sincere.

29. Fasting brings about favor with God.

30. Churches and church leaders will become more efficient in the house of God.

    This book is not only designed for Christians to read. Do not think that because you may not be saved, you too cannot receive any benefits from fasting. If I make you feel that way, it is wrong. However, it is important for me to explain the difference between fasting as a believer and fasting as a nonbeliever. From a spiritual view, the Christian who fasts, will receive spiritual renewing, washing, regeneration, awareness and spiritual blessings. When believers fast, they give their bodies rest from eating any and everything they desire to eat. The best cooks are normally in churches. When we give our bodies a break, the Holy Ghost can enter our temples and start "spring cleaning." He washes our thoughts, rids our bodies of unwanted substances, and renews our mind.

Some individuals, who are not Christians, in contrast, fast for the reason of great physical health and for the ability to stay energetic and enthusiastic. Many more Americans alike are learning that they must take care of their bodies. There is an influx of people across America going to fitness centers. Exercising is one of the best ways to take care of the body, and I should know because I body-build. I have also trained many people in health and physical fitness. Let us look at why fasting is an excellent source for the physical man.

27 Reasons to Fast for Physical Results

The numbers are rapidly growing of those persons that realize, whether they are Christians or not, fasting is one of the greatest causes of the body becoming healed. Doctors treat their patients with this method, to cleanse them from impurities. Some doctors will not allow patients to eat for a period of time, because the body needs to rid itself of all of the waste it has taken in. I have personally instructed people who have had diseases, to fast and fasting has caused the diseases to disappear. Now I am no fool. I truly believe this healing was a miracle from God, but I am also aware that fasting will cause diseases to die. So, you may ask, what will fasting do for my body?

Fasting will clean your circulatory system.

1. Fasting makes recovery faster, after operations.
2. Fasting causes the respiratory system to better exchange carbon dioxide and oxygen with its environment.
3. Fasting improves bowel movement.
4. Fasting improves the heart, and lessens chances of heart disease as well as heart failure.
5. Fasting improves skin complexion and softness.

6. Fasting minimizes energy use, which would ultimately make one more spontaneous and more energetic after a fast.
7. Fasting removes bad temperament and cravings for such things as cigarettes, alcohol, sex, lust, cheating on spouses, and gambling.
8. Fasting makes the body less susceptible to ailments within the body.
9. Fasting brings deliverance from asthma, constipation, diarrhea, and indigestion.
10. Fasting starves lusts of spending excessively, impulsive buying, and unnecessary competitiveness.
11. Fasting brings emotional stability. Thus, when fasting is done correctly, an individual would not do foolish things he will regret later.
12. Fasting purifies the mind, allowing it to think correctly.
13. Fasting will make any person who is aging feel younger.
14. Fasting will bring you longer life.
15. People, who have cancer, tumors, goiters, arthritis, migraine headaches, heart disease, etc., can become totally delivered from these sicknesses. I have known people who have had these illnesses and were delivered as a result of fasting.
16. Fasting will improve patience, which will bring on virtue, temperance, and long suffering.
17. Fasting causes the stomach walls to decrease, which will make the appetite less likely to desire to return to the old eating habits.
18. Fasting will help those that are overweight to reach a normal weight, and those that are small or petite, a normal, healthy size. In other words, small or skinny people can fast also.

19. Fasting will destroy the lust of fornication (sex without being married), adultery (sex with someone outside of your own spouse, or looking at someone other than your spouse and desiring them sexually), inordinate desires (masturbation and unclean passions), uncleanness, evil

20. concupiscence, and covetousness, which is idolatry (see Col. 3:5).

21. Fasting improves your five senses: Touching, Tasting, Hearing, Smelling, Seeing; however it does not improve you in this way to make you become more fleshly, but rather, to bring more awareness to you.

22. Fasting causes demons in a demon possessed person to flee.

23. Fasting will bring about job promotions, salary raises, favor on your job, and the starting of new businesses

24. Fasting will cause personal relationships to improve.

25. Fasting causes us not to sleep too often or excessively. If you are one who could not sleep properly (insomnia), after a fast you will find rest for your body.

26. Fasting will cause the male to have more self control; patience; and to become more outgoing, giving, caring, responsible, vulnerable and thoughtful.

27. Fasting will cause a woman to become sweeter, quieter, more humble, more affectionate, less argumentative, and more resourceful (very plainly put a virtuous woman).

Chapter - 5

Developing a Relationship with God

"By faith Enoch was translated that he should not see death, and was not found, because God had translated him: for before his translation he had this testimony that he pleased God." (Heb. 11:5)

      The most exciting aspect of Christianity for an aspiring man or woman, while pursing their call of God, is to have a personal relationship with the Lord. Being able to communicate with God is not something you can learn from a book, or by attending a seminar on how to hear from God. To hear from God you must push the dinner plate aside, for however long it takes. After the sacrifice of fasting has been made the demonstration of the power of God will begin to occur. Many are taking on the responsibility of preaching the gospel, but some are preaching without a demonstration of power.

Paul said in I Corinthians 2:1-5:

And I brethren, when I came to you, came not with excellency of speech or of wisdom, declaring unto you the testimony of God. For I determined not to know any thing among you, save Jesus Christ, and him crucified. And I was with you in weakness, and in fear, and in much trembling. And my speech and my preaching was not with

enticing words of man's wisdom, but in the demonstration of the Spirit and of Power. That your faith should not stand in the wisdom of men, but in the power of God.

Here, Paul was simply making the statement that all of his words may not have been perfect as he deliberated God's word, neither was he concerned with familiarizing himself with these people. Paul admitted that he may not have known the philosophies they knew, nor was he interested in their religious cliques. His main concern was that of the Lord Jesus Christ, Christ's crucifixion and His resurrection. Paul decided to lay aside religious and philosophical knowledge to receive God's ultimate anointing upon his life. God took a man who completely humiliated the Christians, and used him for His glory. The Lord was only able to accomplish this in Paul's life, however, because Paul submitted to His will. Any person, who will give up his life in the world and allow God to manifest His power in them, will be readily used.

One of the problems we find today is that when God raises up preachers, teachers, and evangelists, they become lifted up with pride and wealth, and succumb to greed and selfishness. The Lord is looking for consistency in His servants. If as many persons hear from God as they claim, they would know that God does not desire for them to become sidetracked by success. What evidently happens is that man has a plan to become successful, and success overrides his commitment to God.

Joshua's Relationship with God

"Have not I commanded thee? Be strong and of a good courage; be not afraid, neither be thou dismayed: for the Lord thy God is with thee whithersoever thou goest." (Joshua 1:9)

What man must understand is that there is good success and bad success. The Lord spoke to Joshua and said:

Only be thou strong and very courageous, that thou mayest observe to do according to all the law, which Moses my servant commanded thee: turn not from it to the right hand or to the left, that thou mayest prosper whithersoever thou goest. This book of the law shall not depart out of thy mouth, but thou shall meditate therein day and night, that thou mayest observe to do according to all that is written therein: for then thou shalt make thy way prosperous, and then thou shalt have good success. (Joshua 1:7-8)

Now here, God was giving Joshua a warning that there would be things, situations, and tribulations that would come to detour him from the plan or standards that had been set for him by his former pastor, Moses. Joshua could not be dependent on Moses's anointing nor on Moses's relationship with God. Joshua had to develop his own personal relationship with God for himself. The Lord was indicating to Joshua, as He does all of us, not to turn to the left hand or the right, but to keep focused on what he had been called to do. In essence, God was saying, I do not have a problem with you becoming prosperous, but if you are going to prosper, prosper correctly by keeping my commandments and staying in fellowship with Me. There is no way possible for one to backslide out of God's will if he is in tune to the Lord at all times. The problem comes when a person stops meditating on the things pertaining to the kingdom and places his focus on "worldly pleasures." God told Joshua that if he meditated day and night upon doing His will, his way would become prosperous, and he (Joshua) would have good success.

God was also conveying to us that if we stay close to Him we too can attain success. If we stray away from Him, however, we will still gain success, but it will be bad success. Good success is success in the Lord, such as healthy relationships, ordered family life, peace of mind, a personal relationship with God, and an end to financial struggles. In this case, your life is terrific, but you still realize that you cannot do anything without God. Products of bad success are a disordered personal life, involving smoking and drinking; and regardless of you being financially independent, because you truly do not know the Lord as your Savior. In other words, your life is disordered; you have not realized who is your source, you have not repented of your sins, and you have not made acceptance of Jesus Christ as you Savior.

Humility is the Key- Abraham

"And said, My Lord, if now I have found favor in thy sight, pass not away, I pray thee, from thy servant. Let a little water, I pray you, be fetched, and wash your feet, and rest yourselves under the tree: And I will fetch a morsel of bread, and comfort ye your hearts; after that ye shall pass on: for therefore are ye come to your servant. And they said, So do, as thou hast said." (Gen. 18:3-5)

Whatever it is that is stopping you from hearing from God, you must give up. Friends, family members, business associates, social clubs, and negative people in church can hinder you from having the relationship you desire to have ith God. You must ask yourself the question, what is more important to me, my relationship with people, which is stopping my sensitivity to God, or my relationship with God.

Now the Lord said unto Abram,

Get thee out of thy country, and from thy kindred, and from thy father's house, unto a land that I will show thee. And I will make of thee a great nation, and I will bless thee, and make thy name great, an thou shalt be a blessing. I will bless them that bless thee, and curse him that curseth thee, and in thee shall all families of the earth be blessed. So Abram departed, as the Lord had spoken to him, and Lot went with him, and Abram was seventy and five years old when he departed out of Haran. (Gen. 12:1-4)

This man very well could have disobeyed the voice of God, and missed his inheritance. However, he made a decision of what was more important to him. Some people cannot be saved because they are worried about what someone is going to think about them or how someone else will feel about it. When the Lord speaks, you have to move according to that which He has spoken to you; if you wait, someone else may come and take your blessing.

It is also important that you do not allow the misunderstanding of someone else to stop your blessing. As I Corinthians 2 says, the carnal mind cannot contain the things that are of God, because they are foolish to him. Thus, there will be people, who will not understand why you left the church that your grandmother brought you up in, or why you give to your church the way you do. All you have to do is let them know you are being obedient to God and not to man. Then you can say your "yea" or "nay" and go your way! You do not owe them any explanations, and the sooner you realize that the better off you will be.

Abraham came from a family of astrologers, so he definitely needed God to move him. In the same way, some people are in traditional family churches, where they are not growing, nor being taught how to have a personal relationship with the Lord. Abraham realized that he needed to leave, thus he packed his bags, took his wife, his nephew Lot, all of their possessions, the souls they had gathered in Haran, and went to the land of promise. Therefore, when your covenant breakthrough comes, know when God is speaking and act on it.

And the Lord appeared unto him in the plains of Mamre and he sat in the tent door in the heat of the day. And he lift up his eyes and looked, and lo, three men stood by him: and when he saw them, he ran to meet them from the tent door, and bowed himself toward the ground. And said, My Lord, if now I have found favor in thy sight pass not away, I pray thee, from thy servant. Let a little water, I pray you, be fetched, and wash your feet, and rest yourselves under the tree. And I will fetch a morsel of bread, and comfort ye your hearts, after that ye shall pass on: for therefore are ye come to your servant. And they said, So do, as thou hast said. (Gen. 18:1-5)

The Lord appeared to Abraham while he was at the door of the tent during a hot day. Abraham looked, saw the three men, immediately identified them, and offered to help them. In general, people have a tendency of becoming more frustrated as the weather gets warmer. Now just imagine if Abraham had been complaining about the heat and why God had allowed him to experience it, he would have missed his blessing. You may wonder, how is it that Abraham could have missed his blessing when he was the one doing all of the giving? When you give, however, you are blessed. Abraham did not mind fetching water for the angels to wash their feet nor getting bread for them to eat. He humbled himself to those who appeared to have been just men; he did not mind being a servant.

It is so amazing that many people including evangelists, ministers, pastors and preachers do not like humbling themselves to cry out to God; perhaps as they did before they became well known. Some lose their spiritual hunger and thirst because they were not ready for what they asked God for. Humility is a word that simply means "to stay low," however, it does not mean that you cannot live a prosperous life. Many of us (ministers, preachers, etc.) before the days of popularity came, understood what it was to fast and pray. Once some made names for themselves, however, they stopped seeking God the way they were taught. What it takes to become successful, it will take that and more to keep that success. People will set you up momentarily, but the Lord will raise you up for life.

The Lord promotes those He feels He can trust. If a person should decide to stop communing with God, it is not that God did not know he would change, He just allowed that individual to see himself for who he really was. No woman desires to be with a man, who at first takes her to nice places and buys her gifts, then after she gets to know him better and lets her emotional walls down, completely changes from light to darkness into a completely different person. God desires to take us out of our father's house and give us our own inheritance, but He wants our relationship with Him to remain the same.

Esther Remembers

"And when Haman saw that Mordecai bowed not, nor did him reverence, then was Haman full of wrath. And he thought scorn to lay hands on Mordecai alone, for they had showed him the people of Mordecai: wherefore Haman sought to destroy all the Jews that were throughout the whole kingdom of Ahasuerus, even the people of Mordecai." (Esther 3:5-6)

Do not allow yourself to go into the King's palace and change. Esther, niece of Mordecai, a Jew who had been carried away from Jerusalem with the captivity of the Jeconian king of Judah (by Nebuchadnezzar), found herself among the maidens that were brought to Shushan, the palace, by Hege, the king's chamberlain. One of these maidens would then be chosen as the new queen. This was due to Vashti's (wife of King Ahasuerus) refusal to display her beauty at a feast that the he had held. Vashti was now going to be replaced by another woman, who could obey the king's order, and not embarrass him in front of his friends. Thus, it was requested that the young, fair virgins prepare themselves for twelve months, with oil, myrrh, and sweet odors in order to go into the king. If the king found a maiden that he could delight himself with, he might not use her as a concubine, but marry her. When it was Esther's turn, she found favor in the sight of all that looked upon her.

Esther was made Ahasuerus's queen, however, he did not know about her Uncle Mordecai, the man lodging by the gate of the king's house, nor her people, the Jews. It is so amazing that this man, Mordecai, who no one bothered with, was at the king's gate paying attention to whatever was going on. On one occasion, he even overheard two men plotting to destroy the king. So, he alerted Esther to this act and the men were swiftly taken care of. He did not do this, however, to become one of the king's pets, nor to receive anything from King Ahasuerus, but rather, because it was the honorable thing to do.

Nonetheless, Mordecai received no attention. King Ahasuerus promoted Haman over all of the princes, but he did not know that this man was evil. Haman planned to destroy Mordecai, along with all of the Jews. When Mordecai perceived all that was done, he tore his clothes, and put on sackcloth and ashes, crying out loudly before the king's gate. Then, Esther's chamberlains came and related to her all that happened. She sent her servant to Mordecai to comfort him and to clothe him, but Mordecai refused them. All that Mordecai could think about was the destruction of his people by this man Haman.

Esther desired to see the king to bring this matter to his attention, but no one was permitted to enter the inner court, if they had not been called by the king. So Esther, a woman reared by a man living on the street, and a woman who rose to the status of a queen, decided to make a difference. She sent word to gather all of the Jews, and told them to fast for three days, not eating or drinking, on her behalf. She said that she and her maidens would do the same. Determined and resolved in her mind, Esther vowed that even if she should perish, she would perish, but she had to see the king. This woman who was blessed overnight, still remembered where she had come from. She knew what it was to stay humble and to seek the face of God for both her welfare and that of her nation.

Esther boldly went into the king's court and he asked what her request was. She responded, 'let the king and Haman come to the banquet that I have prepared for them' (Esther 5:8). Learning of this, Haman joyfully went home and told his wife Zeresh as well as his friends that the next day he alone would be eating with the king and queen as they honored him. During his preparations for the next day, Haman and his friends made a gallow from which to hang Mordecai, because they were sick of him.

That night, the king could not sleep and he demanded the book of chronicles to be brought to him. As he read, he learned that Mordecai previously had foiled the plan of two of his servants, who sought to destroy him (the king). As a result, the king commanded that the dignity and honor be given to this man Mordecai.

After arriving, King Ahasuerus asked Haman what he thought should been done to a man in whom the king delighted. Haman responded that this man should be given the king's royal robe, and one of the royal horses, and a royal crown. The king responded that he liked Haman's idea, saying that it would be done to Mordecai. Haman incorrectly thought these honors were for him which was why he gave King Ahasuerus such good advice.

Haman did not know the best was yet to come. At the banquet, Esther told the king that she and her people had been sold and were to be destroyed. When the king asked who desired to destoy them, Esther answered Haman. Well, the old clique is that, if you make a ditch for someone to fall in, make one for yourself, because you will be the one to fall in.

Due to Esther's humility to seek the face of God, her people were spared and Haman was hung on the gallows he had made for Mordecai. In the end, Mordecai was promoted and placed over the house of Haman. Thus, when a person stays humble and keeps their relationship with God, they remain in the plan of God.

Hannah it's Your Time

Hannah was a woman that could not have any children, because the Lord had shut up her womb. Now if God was responsible for shutting up a womb, He could very well reopen it. From the time she was married, this woman had to share the things she possessed. Never did she know what it was to have her own of anything. She shared her house with Elkanah, her husband, and his other wife, Peninnah. When it was time for Elkanah to pay alms to his family, he would give Peninnah her portion, but he gave Hannah a double portion. He realized that this woman had some issues, and he felt he could give her things to replace her unhappiness. This did not work, however, because she still had a void in her life that needed to be filled.

There came a time when this woman just broke down. Hannah was unable to eat without tears rolling from her eyes. Her husband tried to reason with her, asking, "am I not better than ten men?" Elkanah did not understand, however, that Hannah's situation was bigger than having another man or having possesions in her life. This woman had a cry in her heart that only God could solve.

Hannah's relationship with God had to become greater than it was. If she wanted to move the Lord, she had to get down to business. Many people claim they want God, or desire to have a relationship with Him, but they are not willing to cry out to Him until they get their answers. Some would rather give up, right before the door is opened for them. This woman vowed to God, that if He would look on her affliction and remember her, she would give her child to Him.

Hannah continued praying before the Lord, even while the priest Eli mocked her, thinking she was drunk. Eli could have hindered her breakthrough, but she did not allow him to hinder her. Her purpose was much greater than someone laughing at her or thinking she was crazy. Hannah realized that her time had come. Now she was going to stop crying and sobbing over her bad situation, and change her circumstances. Hannah needed some answers, so she decided she was going to have her own relationship with God, and get a breakthrough for herself. When the priest realized that Hannah was sincerely praying to God, he said, *"…the God of Isreal grant thee thy petition that thou has asked of him." (I Sam. 1:17)*

"Speak Lord Thy Servant Heareth"

"And ere the lamp of God went out in the temple of the Lord, where the ark of God was, and Samuel was laid down to sleep; That the Lord called Samuel: and he answered, Here am I." (Sam. 3:3-4)

Eli was the high priest in Shiloh when Samuel was born. He had also been a judge, of Israel for 40 years. His service to God was indisputable. He, however, was a man who lacked control of his household. His two sons took sacrificial animals out of the house of God and sacrificed the animals for their own purpose. They also slept with the women who went to the tabernacle. As a result, Eli's sons were killed, and when their father received this news, he fell backwards and broke his neck.

Before the time of Eli's death, however, Samuel even as a child had the utmost respect for Eli. He obeyed Eli's orders and learned much from him. This child stayed at the temple with Eli, and would minister in prayer before Lord. As Samuel grew older he developed his own relationship with the Lord, and gained favor with God as well as the people.

Eli had grown old and could no longer keep his house in order, so God had to raise up someone else that would be obedient to His will. The Lord had become completely unhappy with Eli, and thus sent a man of God to tell Eli that it was God who had raised him up to offer sacrifices unto Him and to serve Him forever.

On a certain occasion, while Eli was lying in bed and Samuel was sleeping, the Lord called Samuel. Samuel answered, "Here am I," as he ran to Eli, thinking it was Eli who called him. This happened three times and each time, Eli would tell Samuel to go lie down. Finally realizing it was God, Eli told Samuel, ***"it shall be that if you hear the voice again, say, speak, Lord thy servant heareth" (I Sam. 3:9).*** The Lord called Samuel again, and the young man did as Eli told him. The Lord told Samuel that He would do a new thing, and that everyone who heard this word would have his or her ears tingle. The Lord also revealed to Samuel the disobedience of Eli and the iniquity of Eli's sons, although He did not restrain them from this disobedience. Thus, God revealed the plan He had for Samuel's life notwithstanding the sins of Eli. As Samuel became sensitive to the needs of God and to those of Israel in their conquest over the Philistines, he rose up to become the judge over Israel.

Chapter - 6

Oh, Yes! They Will Change

Let's Change a Nation

"Then I proclaimed a fast there, at the river of Ahava, that we might afflict ourselves before our God, to seek of him a right way for us, and for our little ones, and for all our substance."(Ezra 8:21)

Jerusalem had fallen and the exile of the Jews had become sure. Thus, their hope, which was placed in that system, was completely obliterated. The children of Israel, however, soon realized that God had complete confidence in Zion, and regardless, had made a covenant with David to allow the temple of God to be built. After a decree by Cyrus of Persia in 528 B.C., Jerusalem was restored. This came as a result of the prophet Jeremiah, who prophesied the word of the Lord to Cyrus, which immediately moved him. The Bible declares that if we believe in the Lord, He will establish us, and if we believe in His prophets, we will prosper (II Chron. 20:20). King Cyrus realized that everything he had accomplished had come directly from God. The people that came out of exile were in order with God. Their spirits had been completely changed and they were ready to build the house of the Lord in Jerusalem. They all began to strengthen each other's hands through their giving of gold, silver, and anything that was needed.

It is so amazing that today, so much foolishness is tolerated in the church and order has become almost outdated. People are finding it hard to work together, and the bottom line is that the church is becoming worldly while the world is becoming churchy. We are slowly drifting from the standards of Holiness, but God is a holy God, and He desires for His house and people to be holy. In Ezra 3, the Bible describes that these people came together as one man in Jerusalem. The church must realize, that we already have a fight with the demons of Satan, thus why should we fight one another?

Joshua stood up and told these people that before they could take another step, they should build an altar to offer burnt offerings unto the Lord. Many Christians today act as if the church builds a temple off of good looks, but I object, that it cannot be done! There must be a sacrifice of giving in order to build the vision of your leader and if you believe in his vision, you are going to support it without complaining. Men who were twenty years old and upward came to support the work of God, along with Zerrubbabel and Joshua. The church has the power to change a nation, but we must first put aside the 'big I's' and 'little U's.'

When the people came to set forward the work of God, this was not lip or eye service but it was service done from the heart. Everyone had a particular job to do, and he/she realized the importance of it. In the body, the eye cannot say, "because I'm the eye, I am more important than the ear," nor can the hand say, "because I can touch, I am more important than the foot." The whole body is important to God in order to get His job done. In this case, the builders laid the foundation, the priests came dressed in their apparel with their trumpets in their hands, and the Levites and the sons of Asaph came with cymbals to praise the name of the Lord. Since they had already witnessed the first temple that was built, the elders began to weep and make a loud noise. They praised the Lord in advance, for what He was about to do.

Thus, these people did not praise God because the temple was built, but they magnified Him for the foundation. Once you realize that God has placed a foundation in you through His servants - prophets, pastors, apostles, teachers or evangelists - you might as well start praising Him. It is time for the church to keep revival burning so that when the enemy comes in like a flood, the spirit of God will be delighted to lift up a standard, since a praise would have already been lifted. However, at the greatest level of God's anointing, and when the power of God has just blessed you in your church service, immediately afterwards, the Devil will come trying to tear down everything that you just finished praising God for. The Devil knows that people who magnify God are the people that will posses power.

Here He Comes, but Don't Run

Truly, Satan will come with all of his devices to make you run, duck or hide. You should understand that he uses a great deal to drain you of your stand. The acrostic for the word **FEAR** is **F**alse **E**vidence of that which **A**ppears **R**eal. My point is that the Devil makes a lot of noise, but in fact, he knows that he cannot hurt you at all. The power that he has is the power you allow him to generate when you fall to his temptations.

> ***There hath no temptation taken you but such as is common to man, but God is faithful, who will not suffer you to be tempted above that ye are able; but will with the temptation also make a way to escape, that ye may be able to bear it (I Cor. 10:13).*** The Lord knows you are going to be tempted, but the Devil does not work for himself, he can only do what God allows him to do. The Lord is the boss! That does not mean that God tempts man, because the scripture tell us in James 1:13, that He does not tempt man, neither can He be tempted

with sin. However, when you are tempted, God will always bring you out.

When the adversaries of Judah and Benjamin heard that the children of the captivity built the temple to God, they came unto Zerubbabel saying, "let us build with you." If the Devil was not your friend when you were not doing well, what makes you think he will be your friend now? Some of the greatest preachers and teachers are those that are not known nationally or internationally; they are making a difference where they are. Yet, the moment God raises them up, every other well-known personality has a desire to be in the same pulpit with them. Prior to their fame, however, the same well-known preachers would not have desired to share their pulpits with the lesser-known preachers.

Satan knows just what to do to try to get close to you so that he might make you feel as though he is on your side. These men came saying, "let us build with you, for we seek your God, as you do; and we do sacrifice unto him since the days of Esarhaddon King of Assur." One of the best pieces of advice I can give you when the adversary comes, is that you should say your "yea" or "nay" and go your way. Do not try to reason with the Devil, because he will disrupt the plan of God for your life.

But Zerubbabel, and Joshua, and the rest of the chief of the fathers of Israel, said unto them, you have nothing to do with us to build a house unto our God: but we ourselves together will build unto the Lord God of Israel, as king Cyrus the king of Persia hath commanded us. Then the people of the land weakened the hands of the people of Judah, and troubled them in building. And hired counselors against them, to frustrate their purpose, all the days of Cyrus king of Persia; even until the reign of Darius king of Persia (See Ezra 4:3-5).

Do not compromise your standards just to be popular; you may win people, but lose the favor of God. Zerubbabel and Joshua stood up boldly and told the men, "we have the proper people in place, enough money, and support to get the job done by ourselves." You must stand up boldly and tell the agents of Satan that you are in control, no matter how bad things appear to be. Tell them to have nothing to do with you, your children, your home, your church, or anything that is a part of you! When the Devil realizes he cannot have his way with you, he will try to weaken you and frustrate your purpose. Understand that he would not be the Devil if he did not try to hinder you. Thus, when the Devil fights you, you know that you are on the right track. Alternately, if you never have any trials, or low moments, you need to check yourself, to see if you are truly saved.

However, when he comes, begin to remind him of the scripture, ***"Therefore I take pleasure in infirmities, in reproaches, in necessities, in persecutions, in distresses for Christ's sake: for when I am weak, then am I strong" (II Cor. 12:10).*** Speak the word back to him; do not try to fight him in your flesh. There are demons assigned to frustrate you and your purpose. Do not give in to them. If you find yourself submitting to God's will, and resisting the Devil, before long, he will pack his bags and move to a weaker vessel. Remember, ***"no weapon formed against you, shall prosper" (Isaiah 54:17)***.

The time had then moved to Artaxerxes, King of Persia, who reigned from 464 B.C. to 424 B.C. Rehum and Shimshai, people he knew, wrote letters against Jerusalem to him, accusing the Jews of being religious by rebuilding the rebellious city. During the fifth century, the Persian Empire was plagued with rebellion. Jerusalem had a history of rebellion against foreign powers, dating as far back as during the reign of Hezekiah and Manasseh (See II Chron. 32:33). With this in mind, it would be easy for the king to believe this accusation. So, these agents of Satan argued that if the Jews rebuilt the wall, they would not pay tolls, nor tributes, nor customs, which they claimed would endanger the way the king was viewed. The king persuaded by the letters, gave Rehumand and Shimshai power to stop the work.

Satan will always try to find a buddy to be on his side. When he sees he cannot have his way with you, he will try to find someone to go along with his plan to make you look bad. He knows that if we keep on building, we will become a threat to his kingdom. Thus, he tries continuously to stop us. The more the Devil fights, the more the church must fast and pray to keep him out. It is true that Satan will hinder us or possibly send stumbling blocks in our way, but he cannot stop us. Paul even said, *"Wherefore we would have come unto you, once again; but Satan hindered us" (I Thess. 2:18)*.

Someone Is On Our Side

"Then Darius the king made a decree, and search was made in the house of the rolls, where the treasures were laid up in Babylon... In the first year of Cyrus the king the same Cyrus the king made a decree concerning the house of God at Jerusalem, let the foundations thereof be strongly laid; the height thereof threescore cubits, and the breadth thereof threescore cubits." (Ezra 6:1,3)

As long as you know without a shadow of a doubt your God-given purpose, you should not find yourself swayed by a setback. One must learn to bounce back through diversities. The Bible tells us that the race was not given to the swift, nor the battle to the strong, but unto those who endure. Endurance simply means perseverance: the ability to fall and get back up, or to fail at something and realize you are not a failure, but rather need to try to do it another way. Often people find themselves giving in the minute something happens that they probably have already faced before. This is not endurance. The prophets Haggai and Zechariah did not find themselves with this kind of attitude. They stood up and prophesied the word of the Lord unto Judah and Jerusalem. These men knew they had to make a stand, by speaking God's word and telling the people it was time to start rebuilding. Although the walls around you seem to be coming down, stand uprightly, brace yourself and push those walls back.

What I especially liked most was their initiative; they did not wait on the king's support, they just went ahead according to plan and started rebuilding. While you say you are waiting on God to move for you, and you are praying, you could very well be working. Stop making excuses for failure or inaction. Start seeking God, and move on the plan of God. As I mentioned before, there are three types of people in life:

- ✞ one who makes things happen,
- ✞ one who watches things happen,
- ✞ and the third who does not know what is happening.

If you are willing to go against what the numbers say, you will end up at the top. Just as the prophets started building while they had no one else to help them. If you want someone to help you, try helping yourself first!

As the Jews were building, the governor Tatnai, asked them, who gave them the right to start building this house, and to make up this wall. One thing you must know, you cannot share your goals and dreams with everyone, because they just will not understand. Many times while you are pursuing your dreams, and goals, those who seemed to be with you will question why you are doing what you are doing. Do not listen to insiders or outsiders because they will not understand your vision. Get started anyhow!

The governor wrote to King Darius that these men, who came out of the captivity, were building the house of God. The prophets did not have time to talk nor debate, they said, "we are the servants of the God of heaven, and we are building the house that was built many years ago, which a great king built years ago." These men were taking back that which their fathers had lost.

Then the governor wrote to King Darius, bringing awareness that in the first year of his reign, King Cyrus had given permission to build the house of God. In the past, King Cyrus had told the men of God to take vessels of gold and silver and bring them to the house of God. Tatnai then asked Darius, the present king to search out the truth of this claim.

King Darius put out a decree that they would search the house of archives. In the ancient capital of Media, the scrolls on which the records were recorded were found. As King Darius read the decree of Cyrus, he was in complete awe, seeing that Cyrus actually had commanded that sacrifices would be made unto the house of God, and gold and silver vessels, which Nebuchadnezzar had taken out of the temple at Jerusalem, also be brought from Babylon.

After King Darius read the decree, he commanded that the Jews receive "tribute beyond the river," that they would have an expense allowance, and that their work be not hindered.

When you are serving God with all of your heart and your motives are toward Him, He will support all of your endeavors. Proverbs 3:5-6 says: **"Trust in the Lord with all thine heart; and lean not to thine own understanding. In all thy ways acknowledge him, and he will direct thy paths."** The Jews were not trusting in their own way or trying to fight their own battle, as so many Christians try to do. We say that we will wait on God no matter how long it takes, but when it seems like God is not moving, we sometimes find ourselves helping God out. The Lord just wants us to stand still, seek Him, and wait on Him.

Darius reigned over Persia from 521 to 485 B.C. and was one of the most astute leaders. He continued Cyrus's policy of restoring the home of the Jewish people. In 521 B.C., Darius ordered that the work could continue. If God's people allow the Lord to work on their behalf, they would receive what they need and more. The Jews had so much favor with the king that he decreed if anyone would try to alter his word, timber would be pulled down from his house, and he would be hung thereon (See Ezra 6).

The Lord gets pleasure out of blessing His people. His desire is to give His people the good of the land and to bless them. God is calling for faithful and able bodies that will not sell out to get with the cliques. Never lower your standards to please people, but rather raise them up to the level God desires for them to be. When you compromise in one area of your life, you will find that you will compromise your soul. God blessed His people, so that the governor had to move speedily on the king's decree. God will not share His glory with any man, therefore when God blesses you, everyone will know that you had nothing to do with it.

The elders of the Jews continued to rebuild and they prospered through the prophesying of the prophets Haggai and Zechariah. The temple was finished on the third day of the sixth year of Darius in 516 B.C. The children of Israel, the priests, and the Levites dedicated the house of God with joy. They realized that although the Devil fought them and hindered them for a while, they had won their victory and that victory was indeed very sweet.

Whenever you are going through your trials and temptations, it may not feel well, but learn to count it all joy. When that trial is over you will be able to testify about what God did for you, and your testimony may strengthen someone else. The Bible shows us how the Jews set themselves apart for the work of God and completed the building. After the completion of the building, the Jews consecrated themselves, and then all of the people ate together. Setting priorities in order is very important to God. There is no easy formula to receiving power, except seeking for it. A person who desires power cannot rely on the anointing of their bishop or pastor, he/she must be willing to seek God for himself.

Fasting and prayer is the key to yokes being destroyed in the life the believer. Many people complain about how the Devil fights, but they do not want to do anything to cause him to move. If your desire is for the Devil to get off your back, seriously start fasting and praying and Satan will have to flee.

Favor of God

Ezra was a scribe, a priest and a judge. His purpose was to teach those that were brought into Jerusalem, after they were held captive, how to be committed to God's oracles. At the point of his return to Jerusalem, he immediately gained favor with Artaxerxes I, during his reign in (464-424 B.C.). This man, Artaxerxes I, was the king of Persia and he had given Ezra commission to return to Jerusalem (about 458 B.C.) to restore order among the people of the new community. Ezra was a man that obviously pleased God, because the king granted him all of his desires, according to the hand of God upon his life. The king could not do anything else but bless Ezra, because his steps were ordered by God.

Although, Ezra had witnessed how God blessed him, he remained humble. The Bible indicates that Ezra prepared his heart to seek the law of God, sought God, and then taught those in Israel God's statutes and judgments. He did not receive his blessing and leave the church, as some Christians do, who do not have the right intentions. The more God blessed him was the more Ezra sought God. As Paul said, "if I teach others, and do not abide myself, then I'll become a castaway." Thus, Ezra became a practitioner of his teachings first, then he went down to Jerusalem and taught the people. There are many pulpit preachers, that desire the fame and fortune, but they do not want to live holy or put God first. It is only a matter of time before exposure will come though. You can only minister according to your level of intellect without the anointing for so long, and then all will fail.

We can see examples of this even in the secular world. There are persons that have worked for companies for many years and when they leave their place of employment, they are not able to get a letter of recommendation. That letter gives you support when pursuing new job opportunities. It proves you had found favor with your employer, and during your tenure, you got the job done. In many cases, new employers may not even check your references, because the name of the company and your credentials speak for themselves. Especially if you have a letter of recommendation from the boss.

Ezra received his letter of recommendation from King Artaxerxes. It indicated that all of the people of Israel, the priests, and the Levites could (of their own freewill) go to Jerusalem. King Artaxerxes also financed Ezra's project. The king told him that all of the silver and gold that he could find in the province of Babylon, with the freewill offering of the people, and of priests, offering willingly for the house of their God in Jerusalem, was his. The king also instructed Ezra to buy bullocks, rams, and lambs, with the meat offering, and whatever else he deemed necessary, with the rest of the money. This man trusted Ezra, because he had a life outside of the pulpit. He had proven his faithfulness to God, so now God began to command the blessing to come. The king also commanded the treasurers to give Ezra whatever else he needed. When God's people are obedient to seek His face, if there are building fund projects or finances that need to be met to finance the vision of your church, God will command the banks to give you your loans regardless of credit. If God can command the ravens, and the widow woman to sustain Elijah, He will do the same for us.

One thing about the blessing of God, "it maketh rich and adds no sorrow with it." When God grants favor, it is not only for the preachers, or for the priests, it is for all those that have a will to serve Him. When the Lord blessed Jerusalem, He did not bless Ezra alone leaving out the rest of the church. The king had to recognize that there were others beside Ezra, who were obedient to God and he said, *"Also take notice treasurers don't touch any of the priests, Levites, singers, porters (gatekeepers, ushers), Nethnim, or ministers of this house of God, it will not be lawful to impose toll (taxes), tribute, or custom, upon them."*

The Man of God Is a Judge

"But the carnal man receiveth not the things of the Spirit of God; for they are foolishness unto him: neither can he know them, because they are spiritually discerned. But he that is spiritual judgeth all things, yet he himself is judged of no man."(I Cor. 2:14-15)

Aside from being a priest, Ezra also had the power to judge. Some Christians say, "don't judge me, because you are not my judge, God is!" Don't you know that the power to judge is in the hand of the man of God? He is the person that watches over your soul.

"Let every soul be subject unto the higher powers. For there is no power but of God: the powers that be are ordained of God. Whosoever therefore resisteth the power, resisteth the ordinance of God: and they that resist shall receive to themselves damnation. For rulers are not a terror of good works, but to the evil. Wilt thou then not be afraid of the power? Do that which is good, and thou shalt have praise of the same: For he is the minister of God to thee for good, but if thou do that which is evil, be afraid, for he beareth not the sword in vain: for he is the minister of God, a revenger to execute wrath upon him that doeth evil (Rom. 13:1-4).

t is quite evident that God is calling for the church to humble itself to leadership. We must all find ourselves being subject to those that are higher in rank than us. If you cannot submit to authority, I would question if God is really dealing with you on speaking terms. In other words, so many people today claim God is speaking to them, yet they cannot even obey their pastors. Someone is lying and you may want to do yourself a favor and check to see if it is you.

A person that is crying as one in the wilderness, such as a pastor, is not trying to hinder your life, but is attempting to enhance what God desires to do in your life. The man of God is there for your well-being, teaching you in the admonition of the Lord. However, if you decide to sin or rebel then you should be afraid, because he has the power to speak judgment on you.

Ezra had been given this kind of authority by the king, to appoint magistrates and judges. According to God, whoever would not obey their law would either be banished, have their goods confiscated, be imprisoned, or be put to death. Nonetheless, Ezra was still humble and blessed the Lord for giving him favor with the king, and for the king's finances in his building project in Jerusalem.

Ezra's Journey

"Then I proclaimed a fast there, at the river of Ahava, that we might afflict ourselves before our God, to seek of him a right way for us, and for our little ones, and for all our substance." (Ezra 8:21)

When Ezra journeyed to Jerusalem, he realized that he could not do all of the work by himself; he needed help. No man or woman of God is self-contained. Neither is any person an island. We all need the support of someone else. Thus, Ezra took about 1,500 priests and chief fathers from Babylon to Jerusalem. He also received the support of some of the Levites, and Nethinim for Casiphia. Although, Ezra had favor with the king, he did not mind sharing the wealth, and the blessings with others. There are many cases where some people find themselves doing well, but could care less about those that are around them. As the Lord blesses us, He desires for us to be a blessing to others.

Despite all of his popularity with the king and elders, Ezra, the spiritual leader, realized at the river Ahava, that if he was going to further his ministry he needed to seek the face of God for an answer. The people as well, needed to fast. Ezra acknowledged the power of fasting as the means to receive the right answer from God, so that he might move according to the spirit of God, and not according to the will of his flesh. If you desire to see the hand of God move for you and your household, push that dinner plate aside and start seeking God. Whoever is the spiritual leader in your home, should make a decision (if they desire to see change come) that it is time to seek the Lord through fasting.

When the enemy came his way, Ezra was afraid to ask the king for a band of soldiers and horsemen to help them because he had already received so much. Ezra was carrying silver and gold valued at about $20,000,000. This is probably why he had to seek God; he needed His divine protection on this journey without an escort. Therefore, this man was confused over what he should do. However, he fasted and sought the face of God. After seeking Him, Ezra said God was found. Before this time everything had fallen in place, just the way he desired it to go. Ezra had had the favor of the King Artaxerxes and all of the people, but now the Devil came against him, and he knew it was time for him to rely on God and not man. When you have tried everything, and it all fails, try Jesus. David said in Psalm 34:8, ***"O taste and see that the Lord is good."*** It is so ironic that after God has just finished blessing you and before He sends you on to your next assignment, the Devil will come. You cannot be elevated to a new level, if you cannot pass the first test.

After Ezra and his company sought God, they departed from the river of Ahava with the hand of God was upon them on the twelfth day of the first month. God delivered them from the hand of the enemy, and all such troubles that laid in wait along the way. If you really want to see the hand of God move for you, try fasting, it works!

Chapter - 7

Godly Impact

"And Jehoshaphat the king of Judah returned to his house in peace to Jerusalem. And Jehu the son of Hanani the seer went out to meet him, and said to king Jehoshaphat, Shouldest thou help the ungodly, and love them that hate the Lord? therefore is wrath upon thee from before the Lord." (II Chron. 19:1-2)

Children of God, we must be so careful of the Devil and his devices. He will try to disrupt the peace of God in our lives. Truly every Christian desires to have peace, however, when things are going a little too smoothly, there comes a time when we need to take inventory of ourselves.

The Lord sent Jehu the son of Hanani, to rebuke King Jehoshaphat, for compromising himself by helping ungodly persons (those who hated the Lord). I do not believe the Lord sent Hanani, to Jehoshaphat just because he helped the ungoldly, but more importantly, he helped those that had decided they just did not want God. When God speaks through His prophet, the prophet is not speaking just to have words spoken in the air, but he speaks for people to take heed.

Jehoshaphat immediately put his house in order, and realized the Devil had him compromising. If you are going to live holy, you might as well live completely holy, or else do not try at all. Jehoshaphat went back to the people and corrected his mistakes, thus God became merciful unto him. The Bible tells us that Jehoshaphat brought the people back unto the Lord God of their fathers (see II Chron. 19:4).

However, before Jehoshaphat corrected his mistakes he could not do anything until he set his own heart to seek God. There are many Christians sitting around scratching their heads wondering why things are not working out for them. If they would just take the time out of their hectic schedules to seek God and be honest with themselves, they would often find that the problem is not with others or God, but with themselves. The seer could have spoken, and Jehoshaphat could have rebelled as his father did against the prophet Hanani, but he did not. Thus, this scenario contradicts the old cliché, 'like father, like son.' This is because Jehoshaphat had a mind of his own. This man sought God, and as a result, God led him to establish judges, and to teach the people the fear of the Lord. After appointing Amariah as the priest over the people, Jehoshaphat also encouraged the people informing them that if they were courageous, the Lord would definitely be with them. Therefore, Jehoshaphat was preparing the people and when the test came, the people of God were spiritually equipped. This test would come to find out how strong they really were.

People will not know when to fast if they do not understand the fear of the Lord, and the proper time to seek God. Jehoshaphat chose Levites and priests, that taught the people not to transgress against God and the consequences of it. If more preachers would get back to the Bible and stop trying to be motivational speakers, God would have a greater impact on the lives of His people.

The Lord told the prophet Jeremiah, "***I have not sent these prophets, yet they ran: I have not spoken to them, yet they prophesied.***

But if they had stood in my counsel, and had caused my people to hear my words, then they should have turned them from their evil way, and from the evil of their doings" (Jer. 23:21-22). The prophet of God always had and always will have a message to cause the lives of people to change. The world will not change, however, unless we give them a reason. Today, people are nearly made to believe that they can live any way they choose and still claim to be saved. This is not true.

It is the responsibility of those that have been chosen of God, to speak the righteousness and judgment of Him. Many spiritual leaders become sidetracked, and find themselves out of the will of God, although pleasing men. As finances began to increase, some just cannot handle the success, and they lose focus of their election. There are evangelists that will not go to small churches, nor preach without having an idea of what the honorarium will be before they agree to an engagement. When money becomes the motive for ministering the word, your heart will not be in preaching and seeing souls saved, but rather, it will delight itself in how much can be made. Therefore, money becomes what God calls filthy lucre. The money is filthy because of the scheming and false prophecy used to obtain it. The prophets of old never sold prophecies, but they gladly spoke God's word, because their mandate was from God, and not from the pockets or wallets of the people. Some self-proclaimed prophets are speaking in self with the motive of obtaining money. That is why when an individual asks what God is showing them about him/her, the prophet will make up a false prophesy to make that person feel good. A true man or woman of God should not exploit God to try to win a popularity contest.

It's Time to Fight Back

No matter what circumstances or situations an individual may face, when a person fasts, the Lord will always step in on time. The Devil has a tendency of sending his agents to influence those that are weak to doubt the power of God. However, God always has a way of providing for His people, even though some of them may lack in their faith.

Jehoshaphat, the King of Judah, found himself and his country being invaded by the Moabites, the Ammonites, and other persons that decided to rise up against Judah and Jerusalem. Jehoshaphat had just done a great job of getting the people back to God, but now his faith was going to be tried.

Preachers, remember that whatever you teach your parishioners, you must first be a partaker of. Christians have a responsibility to stay consecrated because we never know when the Devil is going to attack. When Satan, our adversary, is least expected, will be when he will come as a thief in the night. Thus, the church must always be watchful of the Devil. This is the reason that Jesus warned us to watch and to pray without ceasing. To watch and pray means that you are being observant of the spiritual warfare around you, without fighting the wrong source. Often times people battle with themselves or other persons when they should be praying and fasting. Your fight is not ***"against flesh and blood but against principalities and powers, and the rulers of the darkness of this world" (Ephesians 6:12).*** The children of God must learn what it means to pray without ceasing.

How to Pray and Not FAINT

"And he spake a parable unto them to this end, that men ought always pray, and not to faint" (Luke 18:1).

The first thing we must understand about prayer is that there are many different levels of prayer, and many forms of how to pray. In many cases, there is no right or wrong way to pray. Jesus said, ***"Men ought always pray, and not faint"*** or lose heart. Thus, when tempted to give in or to give up, men ought to turn to prayer. Always means never ending. Some argue that even if they were as righteous as the

Pharisees and could pray morning noon and night, they still could not pray without ceasing or pray at all times. However, the Bible says our righteousness exceeds the righteousness of the Pharisees and praying without ceasing is possible. Praying without ceasing is not making a petition, praying for a designated time, uttering words, an attitude of prayer, nor the mental or physical calisthenics of prayer. In this section, we will explore what it means to pray without ceasing. As we learn to do what Jesus told us, to pray and not faint, we will not faint. If we faint, however, it will be because of a lack of prayer.

The way we worship, and understanding true worship has a great influence on our prayer life. We worship in the spirit of holiness (separation). It has nothing to do with how slow a song is, the way we silently think on a song, or the way we lift up our hands. We worship in the beauty of holiness, when our purpose, the reason for which we are sanctified, is fulfilled. The fulfillment of that purpose brings us into true worship, which causes us to pray. The chirping of a bird, or the song a robin whistles, God calls worship. The waves of the sea that billow over the bank, God also calls worship. It is not worship for the wave to whistle a song or for the robin to billow over a bank, because God gave them each a different purpose. You must find out what your purpose is. When you learn what your purpose is and begin to fulfill it, then you will be worshipping in the beauty of holiness. God said, as a result, He will come down and inhabit the praises of His people.

Prayer is the same way. You may have thought that prayer was only kneeling down, folding your hands, enclosing yourself in a "prayer closest," and performing the rudiments of religion, or reciting the Lord's prayer, maybe even in the sanctuary. That is not prayer without ceasing because these forms of prayer will cease.

"God is a rewarder of them that diligently seek him" (Heb. 6:13). In this scripture, God is referring to those people that believe *He is* and diligently seek Him, not to every one. Therefore, if a man does not believe that *God is*, he will not pray, and he will not believe that God will reward his seeking Him, because to this person prayer would be futile. This is the reason many people do not like to pray; prayer has become a rudiment of religion, rather than a meaningful internal experience. When prayer becomes a rudiment of religion, a person will focus on how long a prayer should be, or buy a prayer book to teach them how to pray 'correctly.' God, however, wants our prayers to flow from the heart of a relationship with Him. When that happens, just like with worship, we will not be praying consciously, but unconsciously.

Therefore, prayer and fainting are mutually exclusive; if you are praying you are not fainting, and if you are fainting then you are not praying. In other words, you cannot live without fainting by just being a nice person; you live victoriously by fighting for your salvation through prayer.

Jesus meant that in daily life, we are surrounded by the world, the flesh, the Devil, demons, faithlessness, perversion, hatred, fear, plagues, infirmity, haters of God, disease, and governments that do not fear God, nor His people. Thus, He indicated that the secret to victory was that men ought always pray and not faint.

Here are examples of the responses of those who faint in their daily situations: If someone asks you how your day is going, and you reply, "so, so," then you are fainting. Your day should be better than good, and better than most! If asked, why you get up to go to work each day, and you respond because you need to pay your bills, then, again, you are fainting. If asked, whether your glass is half empty or half full, and you reply half empty, then you are fainting. As a result, you will be discouraged, you will rely on a prayer line to sustain you, and your finances will fail, because you do not recognize the essence of the Christian life. This essence is that is every thing we do, every word we speak, and every action we take, should be motivated by God's kingdom coming and His will being done. When you begin to take on this mentality you will realize that working is a means to an end, but you will have a greater focus in mind and you will benefit from your labor. As God said, if we give, what we give would be given back unto us. You will also be fulfilling the kingdom of God as the scripture notes in Genesis 3:19 when it says men would eat by the "sweat of his face."

To pray is defined as to wish forward; to desire toward the ultimate end. Colossians 3:1 says that we should ***"Seek those things that are above."*** This scripture does not refer to the rapture, heavenly escape, or walking with your head in the clouds. God, however, is trying to convey to us that we should set our minds and spirits to seek the higher and nobler things, thus there will no longer be any question of our will. ***"Whatsoever things are pure, lovely, holy, just, good report, if there be any virtue, power, praise, think on these things, let this mind be in you which was also in Christ Jesus"(Phil. 4:8)***. Therefore, let your mind think of the things above in heaven, not on where you are down here; live down here, but try to elevate your mind to a new level of thinking in which your thoughts, your mind and your emotions are heavenly. You are not bound by the elements of this existence. Thus, your attitude can depict your spirit and mind, through worship, adoration, praise, and godliness. The end result is that your prayer will be 'not my will, but Thy will be done,' and your every action and emotion becomes seeing the Kingdom of God being established. When you go to church, it will not be out of obligation, but rather out of commitment of seeing God's kingdom come.

Hence, prayer is an attitude of the heart that affects our emotions. Whenever someone fails it is because he has departed from the spiritual attitude of prayer. Paul said in Romans 14:17, ***"For the kingdom…is righteousness, peace and joy in the Holy Ghost."*** Thus, when your emotions and thinking is heavenly, you will have peace and joy, but when a person departs from this heavenly state and attitude of prayer, they will faint. Fainting can be compared to paralysis in that when a person faints he is beat, broken down, and cannot move. The reason the Hebrew boys did not faint when they were threatened to be executed by fire, was that they were praying. They prayed before they went into the fire, in the fire and after they came out of the fire. So, we can gather that the way you handle situations, will prove whether you are praying without ceasing. If you are not ready when the adversary comes, he will make you forget everything you ever stood for in church and testified about, and the word will become insignificant to you.

Jehoshaphat was so inundated with his kingly duties that when the enemy came he was unaware and had to be warned. We must always be sensitive in the spirit, especially when things are going well, because Satan is stirring up something to try our faith. The Devil hates seeing the children of God rejoicing, and he will do everything in his power to discourage you, but do not stop fasting and praying, that is the key to yokes being destroyed and burdens being removed.

Jehoshaphat received the warning from his so-called advisors that a great multitude of people was coming to invade Jerusalem from beyond the sea on their side Syria. As a result, Jehoshaphat became afraid. If you allow people and numbers to control who you are, you will be a failure at life. Numbers do not mean anything in comparison to a person that has faith to believe God for deliverance. Unfortunately, Jehoshaphat received and processed this news, it messed him up. Also, do not let anyone drop garbage in your spirit, because when he/she leaves you will be stuck with having to figure out how to solve the situation.

Jehoshaphat had something working on his side, though, he feared God, and he proclaimed a fast. All of the surrounding cities came together to seek God with him. There comes a time, when we all need someone to pray us out of our "jams." You may not be able to fight with your natural hands, but when you have God's hand fighting for you, yours will not be needed. When the Lord fights your battles against your enemies, they will know that it was impossible for you to have gotten yourself out of that situation or won that battle.

This man lost all sense of pride by standing up, regardless of his status as a king, and talking to God. After he made his petition known to God and commanded all of the people to fast, including their little children, God spoke. The Lord spoke through Jahaziel the prophet, and said, ***"Be not afraid nor dismayed by reason of this great multitude; for the battle is not yours, but God's" (II Chron. 20:15).*** The Lord commanded them to the wilderness of Jeruel, because they would not need to fight in the battle. Now you may ask, how in the world can I be in a battle and not fight? When you understand the philosophy behind fighting, which is that the victor is neither the strongest nor the mightiest, but the strongest willed, you too will learn to be victorious without lifting a hand against your enemy. To do this you must first win in your mind, but to win mentally you must be convinced that you are God's champion.

The Lord also told the people to stand still, and watch His salvation. Some church people have an issue when it comes to standing still and watching God move in their lives. Very simply put He means do not move, stay in your place, and do not leave the church you claim He has sent you to. Stand, and be still! Accordingly, you will be excited as you watch God's salvation just illuminate you.

Then the Lord commanded them not to be dismayed. A dismayed person is sad or distraught by what he may see or experience. Thus, not to fall into this category your mind must be made up, and you must not be fixed on what you see. The Devil knows that if he can have you concentrating on your problem(s) rather than God's given solution, then he can take over your mind. Thus, the Bible warns us to guard our hearts and our minds. When you are not dismayed, no one can pull you away from what God has spoken to you, because you are completely encouraged. Your heart is fixed, and your mind is made up.

Jehoshaphat along with all of Judah bowed to the ground and sought God. Bowing is a sign of humility, and Jehoshaphat displayed this humility, as he did not care about his position as king. Jehoshaphat desired a breakthrough for himself and the people and would stop at nothing to get this breakthrough. The Lord loves when we bow down to Him and although we are bowing outwardly, inwardly we are standing up. When your heart is right towards the things of God, you rise up early in the morning with Him on your mind. Therefore, all of Judah rose up early and went to the wilderness of Tekoa. Even though you may be in the wilderness, when the Lord is on your side, you are still not alone.

Jehoshaphat's job was to prepare the people and he did it, by directing them to believe in the Lord their God. He said, ***"believe in the Lord your God, so shall ye be established; believe his prophets, and so shall ye prosper" (II Chron. 20:20)***. It is so apparent most times that when people go to battle, they invest in the best artillery to make sure the job will be done correctly. Jehoshaphat consulted with the people and they appointed the best singers unto the Lord, who would praise Him in the beauty of His holiness, as they proclaimed, "praise the Lord, for his mercy endureth forever." Then the people began to sing and praise the Lord.

As result, God set ambushes against the children of Ammon, Moab, and Mount Seir, who had risen up against Judah, and they were smitten. It was all due to their hearts turning to God with fasting and prayer as a nation of people (II Chronicles 20).

Chapter - 8

His Power Is Alive

Fasting Touches the Heart of God

"Speak not thou in thine heart, after that the Lord thy God hath cast them out from before thee, saying, For my righteousness the Lord hath brought me in to posses this land: but for the wickedness of these nations the Lord doth drive them out from before thee." (Deut. 9:4)

    The Lord spoke to the Israelites and told them that they were going to pass over Jordan; also saying they would enter and possess nations greater than themselves. Oftentimes, the Lord will speak to His people, but His words enter in one ear and exit out of the other. You may ask, what are you saying? I mean, The Lord will speak His word, and soon thereafter difficult situations will arise, which will cause some to forgot God's words. Some of the Christians that have just finished speaking in other tongues, jumping, and shouting, are those who when faced with adversity, forget God's word.

    The Lord distinctively described the type of people Israel was going to face. He told the Israelites that if they looked at the obvious, indeed these nations were mightier than them. The enemies' cities were fortified to the heavens, and they themselves were great and tall, because they were Anakims. The Lord also told Israel, that they were familiar with their enemy. Every trial and situation you face is already known to you; it is nothing new. *The Bible says, "**Wherefore let him that thinketh he standeth take heed lest he fall. There hath no temptation taken you but such as is common to man: But God is faithful, who will not, suffer you to be tempted above that ye are able; but will with the temptation also make a way to escape, that ye may be able to bear it (I Cor. 10:12-13).***

In order for God's people to be strong, they must be tempted. Temptations come to all people, so do not feel you are the only one that is being tempted. You are not the first and you will not be the last. There are many that have resisted and overcome temptations, so can you. Just as God had always made a way of escape for Israel, He will do the same for you. The Lord advised Israel about their familiar allies, and then He informed them that they were going to overcome that which appeared mightier, and greater in number. The Lord spoke to Moses to tell Israel that He would go before them as a consuming fire, and would destroy the Anakims.

It is amazing though, how soon people forget that it is the Lord that gives us power to gain wealth, and to overcome our enemies. God said He would destroy the Israelites' enemies not because of their righteousness nor their perfect hearts, but rather, due to the wickedness of those nations. God desires to bless His people with the good of the land, but He does not want us to think that it is because of our knowledge, our holiness, or our connections. He does it out of the graciousness of His heart. When the Lord blesses His people, it is because He understands that we are not perfect, but are striving to come into a state of perfection.

Later, God told Israel through the mouth of Moses, that they were not getting the land because of their righteousness, for they were a stiff-necked people. A warning always proceeds destruction. There is not a single person that does not receive a warning before they fall into sin, make bad decisions, or backslide. Moses spoke to Israel about their disobedience to God, and when he went into the mount of Horeb to receive the tables of the covenant, the Israelites provoked God to wrath. God was angered to the point that wanted to destroy them.

Moses stayed in the mountain for forty days and forty nights, neither eating bread, nor drinking any water, but fasting. Moses proved his unselfishness to seek God through fasting and prayer, not for himself, but for the Israelites and their disobedience. God could verily well have destroyed Moses for even confronting Him, because He was completely enraged with Israel. Nonetheless, although God was upset with Israel, He still delivered unto Moses the commandments with the hope of the Israelites repenting. ***"For his anger endureth but a moment; in his favor is life; weeping may endure for a night, but joy cometh in the morning" (Ps. 30:5).*** Moses realized that God was angry with Israel, but he believed that if he approached God with the right spirit, the heart of God would change. This man sacrificed his own flesh to see a nation of people receive deliverance.

I believe even now, if more people in the 21st century church of God would fast and seek God's face, our churches would accelerate in souls being set free, deliverance would be an ongoing cycle, financial struggles would be over, and God would meet every need with surplus.

After this, God told Moses to get out of the mountain quickly because the people had corrupted themselves, turning aside from Him to make themselves a molten image to worship. The old saying is 'when the cat is away, the mouse will play.' If the world does not want to discipline itself, at least we, the body of Christ, should. Today, however, as soon as some pastors leave their congregations, several members are not faithful to church. The problem is that too many people are acting as if their pastors are the ones who have saved them.

Whether or not your pastor or leader is out of town, you should love God enough to serve Him, not to please man, but God. Of course, the pastor loves to see his church full of souls when he is present, but he also desires for the souls to remain faithful to God even in his absence.

Moses had gone on a sabbatical leave to hear from God, and to further the ministry for Israel. The Israelites, however, could not maintain their place without a man watching over them. If your salvation goes only as far as your pastor seeing you, you are not truly saved, and you do not have a relationship with God. We should serve God rather than man, because the Lord monitors your steps, not man. God is the one always watching; He never sleeps nor slumbers.

The Lord's wrath was kindled as God told Moses to leave Him alone so that He could destroy Israel. The Lord told Moses I am able to build you a people from ground level, mightier and greater than they are. However, there was something about the Israelites that impeded Moses from turning his back on them. It may have because he was Hebrew by nationality, or that he had seen how far God had taken them, or the fact that he saw God send over 600,000 people across the dry ground of the Red Sea. Whatever the reason, Moses had decided he would not give up on Israel, and did not want God to build a new nation of people.

If we look at it for what it is worth, Moses would have had it easier, starting off with new people. Many sales organizations, believe that it is easier to train someone new on a system, because they do not have a "know-it-all-tendency," unlike salespeople who have sold for a long time, who are set in their ways. In many cases, you cannot teach an old dog new tricks, but you can a puppy. Moses, believed in those that were from 'the old school,' so he left the mountain of Horeb and reproved Israel. In his anger, though, he broke the two tables of stones upon which were written the Ten Commandments, and fell down before God with forty more days of fasting and prayer.

Meanwhile, God was so angry that while Moses was descending the mountain, it burned with fire. Moses admitted to Israel, he was afraid of the anger of God, but nonetheless, the Lord spared them. You see, even if the Lord is upset with what you have done, if you start fasting and praying, you can move the heart of God.

An organization's success or failure is due to management. Now in our profession as preachers of the gospel, we realize our total success is dependent on how we live our life towards God. When a church grows, it is due to the anointing on the life of the preacher, and those that are in leadership who have caught the vision. The Lord also wanted to destroy Aaron, the leader in charge of the people in Moses's absence, but because Moses sought the face of God, the Lord spared him. If it had not been for the weakness and lack of faith on Aaron's part, Israel would have kept their place in Moses's absence. All pastors across this nation make sure that if you have someone as an assistant pastor, he has the same mind as you have! If not, that person can destroy your vision in the matter of minutes. There can only be one head and all of the rest are helpers, assistants, helpmeets, etc. The Lord has never assigned two people to lead at one time; He only uses one leader at a time.

Moses told Israel, that even when they were at Kibroth-hattaavah, they had provoked God, as well as when He sent them to Kadesh-bernea. God told them to go and possess the land, and they rebelled. Many times God wants to bless you, but if you already have your way of doing things, He cannot move for you, and that is rebellion. Remember, rebellion is as the sin of witchcraft. Moses told Israel, "I had to touch the heart of God that time also, by fasting for forty days and nights, or otherwise He would have destroyed you." Moses did this by refreshing God's memory of his covenants with his servants, Abraham, Isaac, and Jacob, and turning God's focus away from the stubbornness, the wickedness, and the sins of the people. Moses knew the right words to move the God. He knew he needed to fast before God's presence, not eating nor drinking anything.

Today, people fast drinking orange juice, tea, and even coffee. That is not the ordained fast that **destroys** every yoke. It will only **break** some yokes, which makes it possible for the broken yokes to be reformed on your life. That is a reason why your flesh will continue to rise; it is not being denied, that which it loves. However, if you want to move the heart of God and destroy those yokes, try fasting for several days, without eating or drinking anything except water.

Jesus Touched the Father

"And when they were come to the multitude, there came unto him a certain man, kneeling down to him, and saying, Lord, have mercy on my son; for he is a lunatic, and sore vexed: for oftimes he falleth into the fire, and oft into the water, And I brought him to thy disciples, and they could not cure him." (Matt. 17:14-16)

Everywhere Jesus went, there were persons waiting for Him to come to their town, because they realized He had power and favor with the Father. Although He had great influence with the Father, it was only due to His own personal relationship with Him. Unlike today, when Jesus came into His ministry He sought the power of His father immediately. Today on the other hand, preachers say they want power, but they do not want to do what it takes in order to receive this power. Jesus was baptized, and fasted forty days and forty nights, without eating anything. He was willing to lay aside His occupation, not communicate with friends, and disassociate Himself from people to seek the will of His Father. I can imagine His body went through weakness and pain, but He never gave up, because He also new He was setting an example for you and I.

Like a son that desires to excel in whatever he does to impress his father, Jesus wanted to make His father proud of Him as well. Jesus found Himself in a new position; He did not know sin and He was never poor. Fortunately, by Him passing His test, He proved that He did not have to fall to sin, nor the Devil's temptation, and that He truly was the Son of God. Jesus's temptation showed us that He was human, and He gave us an example to follow. Jesus fasted to prove to us that if you truly want to defeat the Devil you should not walk around sad or crying, but you can defeat the enemy by fasting. TRY FASTING, IT DESTROYS YOKES!

Satan made a statement, "If you are the Son of God, change these stones into bread." But Jesus told him, "No. It is written that man shall not live by bread only, but must feed off of the word of God." Then Satan came back a second time and said, "If you are the Son of God, jump off this pinnacle, for the scriptures say, He shall give his angels charge concerning thee: and in their hands they shall bear thee up, lest at any time, thy dash thy foot against a stone." Jesus responded, "It is written thou shalt not tempt the Lord thy God." Jesus was going through several tests by the Devil. He was taken on a spiritual rollercoaster ride to prove to us that the Devil will tempt you, but you do not have to fall. After this fast, Jesus began to see immediate results of why the Devil came to tempt Him. If you allow Satan to stop your purpose, you will never know the people's lives you would have impacted, so do not stop fasting and praying.

When Jesus had come to the mountain, a huge crowd was waiting for Him. A man came and kneeled down before Him, asking for mercy. The man admitted his son was having seizures and was suffering terribly. Apparently, the Devil was having his way with the boy, throwing him in fire and then sending him into the water for consolation. The man said, "I brought him to thy disciples, and they could not heal him." We must remember Jesus had already given His disciples power over unclean spirits (to cast them out), power to heal the sick, and power to raise the dead, if it were necessary. Yet, the disciples encountered this boy with this condition, and could not anything about it.

When God has chosen for your life to be used, if you should get out of your place and you cannot feel the presence of God, do not blame it on a bad day, or on God not wanting to use you. NO! It is your fault, because you lacked the discipline to seek the face of God. Jesus told the disciples and those that heard Him speak, "you are a stubborn and faithless people!" Fed up, He wanted to know how long He was going to have to be with them, watching over their every move, although He already told them what to do. Similarly, some Christians just do not want to grow up, and as long as they know they have someone to run to with their problems, they will never mature. What you have to do is correct them and show them where they are making mistakes.

Jesus told them to bring the boy to Him. He rebuked the Devil, and the Devil had to flee from the boy; immediately the boy was healed. Afterward, the disciples came to Jesus privately, and asked, "Why couldn't we cast out the demon?" Jesus pointed out that they did not have enough faith, saying, if they had as much faith as a grain of mustard seed, they would have been able to speak to a mountain, and it would move. Thus, nothing would have been impossible for them. Then He went on to tell them that this kind of demon also would only come out through fasting and prayer.

There are certain situations you will find yourself in, where the only person that can help you is you! Making a sacrifice to push the breakfast, lunch, and dinner plates aside, then falling on your face to seek God, will be the only answer. Many people say they fast, but are lying to themselves. True fasting is God's ordained fast. Today, many do not like the old way of fasting or the ordained fast, because they say it is 'played out.' The old way is not 'played out,' but what happens is that man has thought of an easier way to get around waiting and fasting. Things are made to assure and comfort the flesh. The flesh has to die, and if it does not die now, the soul will die later. If you say you want to have influence and power with God, do not be afraid to make the sacrifice to seek for it. There are many Christians today, who fast drinking orange juice, tea, coffee. That, as mentioned before, is not the fast that the Lord has ordained, that is what man has decided he wants to do. God's fast is going to destroy yokes and let every person that is oppressed go free.

Mary Come Out, the Master's Here!

"Jesus said unto her, I am the resurrection, and the life; he that believeth in me, though he were dead, yet shall he live; and whosoever liveth and believeth in me shall never die, Believest thou this?" (John 11: 25-26)

The Bible says that Jesus loved Martha, her sister, and Lazarus. However, although He loved them, there would still be some things that would occur in their lives, which they would not have the answers to. Their brother Lazarus died, and they could not fathom why this would happen to him. After all, Lazarus was a good Christian person that obviously had favor with the Lord. Some would even ask, if Jesus loved Lazarus so much, why would He have allowed Lazarus to die?

When the sisters sent a message saying that their brother was sick, they completely believed in their hearts that if Jesus was around, Lazarus would not be as sick as he was, and he certainly would not be on his deathbed. Obviously, Lazarus's sickness was something that happened suddenly, catching them off guard. When the news got to Jesus he said, "this sickness is not unto death, but for the glory of God, that the Son of God might be glorified thereby" (John 11:4).

There are sicknesses, financial obligations, losses of opportunities, and miracles that will occur in your life for the glory of

God, that He might prove His power is indeed alive. There are those, however, who instead of putting their confidence in God, seek for man to give them consolation. What they do not realize, though, is that man is not the one that can save or deliver them. What should they do? TRY CALLING ON THE NAME OF THE LORD! Jesus's response was not that Lazarus would not die, but that he would live.

Although Jesus loved Martha, Mary, and Lazarus, He stayed where He was for the next two days and did not go to them. My God, this must have seemed out of order to them; Jesus must have been in the flesh! Martha and Mary must have said, whom does He think He is not coming when we call Him? That is the typical response by some Christians when they call for their pastors and do not get a response, or when they ask someone to do something and it is not done when they desire for it to be done. What you must realize is that God's timing is different from that of man. He does not always move when you want Him to move, rather, He moves when he desires. In other words, the Lord moves in your life when you open up yourself for Him to move. God cannot move for you if you are crying, because you cannot see clearly; while you are complaining, because you will not hear Him; and after you have told everyone else what you are dealing with, because He wants to see if you are disciplined enough to come to Him for yourself and be willing to wait for that which you asked for.

As I have said, many people do not like to wait. Some want a job when they snap their fingers, others want healings right away, or need houses immediately and cannot see why God will not move on their demands without delay. You see, the Lord knows what is best for you, and if He has not given it to you yet, it is because either you are not ready for it, He has something better in store for you, or the timing is not right.

"Knowing this that the trying of your faith worketh patience." (James 1: 3)

"For ye have need of patience, that, after ye have done the will of God, ye might receive the promise." (Heb. 10: 36)

"Wherefore seeing we also are compassed about with so great a cloud of witnesses, let us lay aside every weight, and the sin which doth so easily beset us, and let us run with patience the race that is set before us. Looking unto Jesus the author and finisher of our faith, who for the joy that was set before him endured the cross, despising the shame, and is set down at the right hand of the throne of God." (Heb. 12: 1-2)

These scriptures were placed here so that you can study them, because it is going to take patience when you have started to grow as a Christian, to wait for your change to come. Do not give up or give in, but I say wait!

Jesus allowed two days to pass, and then He told the disciples that they would go to Judaea again. However, He still did not seem to be tearing down doors to get to Lazarus. Strangely, Jesus told the disciples that their friend Lazarus had fallen asleep, so He would go and wake him. Although, Jesus did not mean to startle them, the disciples were confused because they did not understand what He meant. The disciples did not know any better, so they thought that based on what Jesus said, Lazarus was getting better and needed to recuperate. Then Jesus plainly had to tell them that Lazarus was indeed dead, and that He was glad He was not there, with the intent that they might have another opportunity to believe.

We can clearly see here, that there are obstacles in our lives that will hopefully cause us to have faith in God and not faint out. The child of God should realize that out of every trial will come victory, and out of every bad situation will come good, so that God will get the glory. Ask yourself, when tribulations and trials come do you murmur, dispute, complain, and blame, or do you trust, believe, have faith, and never doubt? The disciples were reluctant to go because they knew danger lay ahead of them; they even tried to talk Jesus out of going. Conversely, Thomas, the doubter, stuck with Jesus's ministry when the others out of fear did not. Thomas boldly said, 'let's go and die with Jesus.'

If Jesus had been with Lazarus, while he was dying, because of His love for the family He probably would have healed Lazarus as opposed to letting him die. However, there was a greater purpose. Lazarus's death proved that Jesus could not only heal the sick, but also had power over death. When Jesus got to Bethany, Lazarus had already been in the grave for four days. It was a custom of the Jews, when someone died to bury them the same day, and not wait for family members to come from out of town, unlike today. Many people came to Lazarus's funeral service to pay their last respect, but it is so amazing, how God can take something that seems so negative and allows other persons to be present when He shows up with a miracle.

THIS HAPPENS THAT OTHERS WHO DO NOT BELIEVE WILL BELIEVE!

Martha came out of the house to meet Jesus when she heard that he was there but Mary stayed in the house. Mary could have stayed back for various reasons. Maybe she was upset with Jesus that He waited so long to come when her brother was dead. After all, they did not need Him since Lazarus was dead. She could also have thought He betrayed them and was not a true friend, since a real friend would have been there when they needed him.

Martha on the other hand was operating in faith. In John 11:21, Martha in essence told Jesus, "Lord, I wish you had been here, and my brother would have not died. But even now, I know that God will give you whatever you ask." Jesus told her that Lazarus would rise again and thinking He meet during the last days, she said she knew he would rise again in the resurrection. Jesus then replied, "I am the resurrection, and the life; he that believeth in me, though he were dead, yet shall he live: And whosoever liveth and believeth in me shall never die, Believest thou this?" Martha shouted, "Yes, Lord I believe that thou art the Christ, the Son of God, which should come into the world." After Martha gave Jesus her response, she ran to the house and told Mary that the Master had come, and was calling for her. After Jesus asked where Lazarus was laid, He began to weep, and the people realized that He truly loved Lazarus. There is something that also strikes me about this scripture, these women, although Jesus came four days later, never questioned why He came late nor His authority. That is something Christians everywhere should take note of. Do not question the authority of your leader; respect them.

When Jesus told the people to remove the stone, and Martha said the body would stink, but Jesus asked, 'didn't I tell you to believe, and you will see the glory of God?' Jesus prayed to the Father, and after He was finished He said, "Lazarus come forth." Jesus commanded the people as Lazarus was rose, to take the bandages and burial clothing from his face and body, because they were for the dead. In essence, Jesus meant loose him, and let him go. If you are patient and wait on God, you too will witness His power in operation for your life! Jesus had stored up much fasting and prayer for times like this, therefore, the Father had to honor His prayers.

Apostle. Dr. P.W. Reed, Ph.D.

Chapter - 9

Let's Break Out with Power

"In those days I Daniel was mourning three full weeks. I ate no pleasant bread, neither came flesh in my mouth, neither did I anoint myself at all, till three whole weeks wee fulfilled." (Daniel 10:2-3)

The Wisdom of God Is Obtained Through Fasting

There is a complete difference in our walk with God when we fast verses when we do not. A person that fasts will find himself in a place with God where visions and dreams will begin to be opened up to their understanding. During a fast, you will find that your spirit is very sensitive to things around you through your senses of hearing, seeing, touching, smelling, and tasting. Now I do not mean hearing people, or tasting food, but rather hearing from God and tasting more of His goodness. The hunger inside of you will be stirred up. The Bible teaches us to stir up the gift of the presbytery. Believe me, when a person goes on an extended fast they are stirring up the anointing in their life.

Daniel found himself standing by the river Hiddekel. As he looked, he saw a man clothed in linen, and girded with fine gold uphaz. He saw a body like unto beryl, with a face as bright as lighting, eyes as lamps of fire, arms and feet the color of fine brass, and the voice of a multitude. There were other men around Daniel but they did not see this vision. Although they experienced the quaking under their feet as Daniel did, they did not stand still, but fled to hide themselves. Daniel was in position to hear from God, but possibly his friends were not. There are people you will deal with on a daily basis that are not serving God with all of their heart as earnestly as you are. Therefore, do not expect for them to understand you when you communicate with them about things pertaining to spirituality. Your so-called friends may like you in the beginning, but once you become caught up with God, they will run because you will become too deep for them. In essence, those friends will like you as long as you can conform to their ways. When you do not, you will find that you really do not have any friends but Jesus.

"But the natural man receiveth not the things of the Spirit of God for they are foolishness unto him, neither can he know them, because they are spiritually discerned… For who hath known the mind of the Lord, That he may instruct him? But we have the mind of Christ." (I Cor. 2:14-16)

As you get closer to God, you will find yourself segregating from people. It is easier to hear from God when you are alone. Sometimes being alone does not feel pleasant, however the benefits of being in God's presence cannot be measured. The vision was so awesome that it affected him physically as well as spiritually. Physically, Daniel had no strength in him, and his comeliness was turned into homeliness. Daniel found himself in a deep sleep with his face and body on the ground. The anointing of God is so strong that it removes all flesh, and as you exert yourself for God, you will find your rest is much better under this anointing. When you truly love God, it is hard to praise Him in self. Someone told me years ago, "if you want God to really bless you, try getting ugly for him." I find that simply means let your self go! It is not about facial expressions, or being loud. Letting yourself go means allowing the spirit of God to have His way in your life. The life of a person that fasts reflects their not minding God using them for His glory.

This vision was so magnificent that a hand lifted Daniel up and set him on his knees and on the palms of his hands. In this instance, Daniel's friends ran away from him, at the presence of God. When all of your friends run out on you because you have decided to follow the Lord, realize, He will not leave you in a rut or flat on your face for people to walk around and laugh at you. He will always come and pick you up. Even if you fall, He will forgive you of your sins, for the Lord is faithful and just.

After this, Daniel began to hear the voice of the Lord speak to him, and he trembled in his shoes. Fasting will give you an open line of communication with God, because spirit is dealing with spirit. Thus, you must expect God to talk with you when you are least expecting Him to and you must be in place to hear from Him when He speaks. I do not believe every person is hearing from God as he/she may say. God's voice is so powerful that it does make you afraid when first hearing it, because it is a voice you have never heard before. There are so many people lying on God saying He speaks to them, when in reality it is their own mind telling them what to do. When the Lord speaks to you about doing a particular task, it will not cause you to lose out on what you say He has blessed you with. In other words, if you claim that God told you to go out and purchase a new car, a year later, there will be no struggles in trying to hold unto it nor fear of repossession.

If the Lord really speaks to as many people as claim He does, we would see less corruption in our churches, and more preachers and congregations in order with God. We would not see nor hear about cliques in the church, backbiting, or hypocrisy. All of this is due to the lack of seeking the face of God.

I find today people go to church to socialize or to see who they can become their friends. The church is not a social club. If you have ever said you want to be like Jesus, you must go to your secret hiding place, where no one else is, and cry out to God. If you push the breakfast, lunch and dinner plates aside, and feast off the heavenly food for a day, I promise there will be a change in your walk with the Lord. Fasting takes discipline, and that is an area where many people find themselves lacking. If you cannot discipline yourself not to eat for 12 hours, how can you be trusted to run an organization or manage people, since you obviously cannot manage yourself? Fasting calls for self-management. It is much easier to tell someone else what not to do, but would you be able to do what you ask them not to do?

Daniel chastened himself before God; therefore, his words were honored in the sight of God. Fasting gives you honor with God provided it is done with the right intent. Daniel was so well respected, because he sought the face of God that the angel came to make known unto Daniel what would happen to the people in the latter days. Do not be shocked when God speaks back to you after you have given yourself holy unto Him. The vision was so dreadful, that Daniel fell upon his face again, and asked the angel how he could talk with him, since he (Daniel) had no strength within him. In response, the angel just touched Daniel and gave him strength. That is what we need in our churches today, the Lord to give us a touch to just become drunk in the spirit. When you are drunk in the spirit, you loose yourself in His anointing. It takes a while to come down when you are caught up in the spirit, and the Lord has to release His anointing from you gradually, so that you can function properly. So, the angel strengthened Daniel, and told him that he was going to fight with the prince of Persia, but then the prince of Grecia would come. The angel was showing Daniel that he was preparing him for the fight the enemy was about to bring him, and encouraging Daniel that nonetheless, he would have the power to stand.

Chapter - 10

Can I Make a Difference?

"Then came to him the disciples of John, saying, Why do we and the Pharisees fast oft, but thy disciples fast not? And Jesus said unto them, 'Can the children of the bridechamber mourn, as long as the bridegroom is with them? but the days will come, when the bridegroom shall be taken from them, and then shall they fast'." (Matt. 9:14-15)

Let us make sure we understand what Jesus was really saying here. He was not saying that in the times we are living in today, we do not need to fast. What He was asking the disciples of John was whether guests mourn while the bridegroom is there with them? The answer would have been no, because while the bridegroom (Jesus) was with them, He was the one fasting so that yokes could be destroyed on the lives of the people. Jesus responded, obviously because they did not give Him an answer. He replied, "someday the bridegroom will be taken away, and then shall they fast."

Well the bridegroom is here in spirit, but not in flesh. We must now fast to operate in the power that He demonstrated. Although Jesus in Matthew 10, gave the disciples power to heal the sick, raise the dead, and give sight to the blind, they still had to seek for the authority to exercise it after He left. The Bible says in Galatians 6:4, ***"But let every man prove his own work, and then shall he have rejoicing in himself*** *alone, and not in another."* Paul meant here that a man should learn to do things for himself and he would enjoy the personal satisfaction of having done his work well. As a result, he would have no need to compare himself to anyone else because we are all responsible for our own conduct. Any person that wants to make a difference or is striving to do their best, feels extremely good when they see the results or their accomplishments. There is great truth in the notion that men are highly competitive, and hate to see themselves fail. However, life is greater than a sport competition, it is a revolving door, and everyone has to do their part in order for that door to continue to turn. There should not be a person that passes and on their tombstone the words "Not Used Up!" appears where their name should be.

Every preacher should make a difference in his local community, by winning souls. There should be a distinct mark (works) that he or his ministry is known for. Every evangelist should make a difference as they are out on the road ministering at different churches, revivals, and conventions. If souls are not being added to the kingdom, but rather a lot of money, you are not a true evangelist. Prophets make differences in the lives of people, because when they are in true counsel with God, they cause people to hear God's word, and these people in turn will turn from their evil ways and doings (see Jer. 23:21). The bishop can make a difference by setting the churches, which are under his covering, in order. There should not be cliques, mess, or whoremongers in the house of God. The effective apostle would set up churches on a national and international level, because he knows ministry is greater than just where he is. Thus, everyone can make a difference.

So, do you want to know how you can make a difference? Let me tell you how!

"For the Lord has driven from before you nations great and strong: but as for you, no man hath been able to stand before you unto this day. One man of you shall chase a thousand: for the Lord your God,

he it is that fighteth for you, as he hath promised you." (Joshua 23:10)

"And you shall chase your enemies, and they shall fall before you by the sword." (Lev. 26:7)

What I like about a person that desires to make a difference is that all he/she must do is show up with the Lord on his/her side and leave the situation in God's hands, He will do the rest. Joshua reminded Israel that the Lord had driven out great and powerful nations before and He would do it again. Because we have the Lord, who is greater than any nation, on our side, one anointed and God-appointed individual will chase or drive away a thousand of their enemies, for God will back this individual up and join him in the fight. Every believer must realize they do not have to fight in the battle to win, just show up. Many Christians talk about how they have been fighting the Devil all week long. If that be the case, they are wearing themselves out in a hopeless situation with an entity that is already defeated. Why fight a devil that has been whipped by your big brother Jesus? Paul told Timothy *"Fight the good fight of faith, lay hold on eternal life, whereunto thou art also called, and hast professed a good profession before many witnesses" (I Tim. 6:12).* Thus, the only fight you should be fighting is the fight of faith, which is not with the Devil, because he is already defeated.

And five of you shall chase an hundred, and an hundred of you shall put ten thousand to flight: and your enemies shall fall before you by the sword. For I will have respect unto you, and make you fruitful, and multiply you, and establish my covenant with you. And you shall eat old store, and bring forth the old because of the new. And I will set my tabernacle among you and my soul shall not abhor you. And I will walk among you, and will be your God and ye shall be my people. (Lev. 26:8-12)

How shall one chase a thousand, and two put ten thousand to flight, except their Rock had sold them, and the Lord had shut them up?

Therefore, when your enemy comes, if you are prayed up and have fasted, he cannot touch you at all. God said in the scripture above, that we will chase down all of our enemies and slaughter them with the sword. Five of us will chase a hundred, and hundred of us will chase ten thousand! Our enemies will even fall beneath the blow of our weapon. God will place His favor upon your life and will cause you to multiply and be blessed, just to bring this covenant to pass. A sincere desire to make a difference will cause God to give you surplus of crops or natural abundance. As a result, you will have so much you will have to get rid of the leftovers from the previous year to make room for each new year's harvest.

You Can Make a Difference

Many people are not aware of the fact that they can fast on the behalf of someone else. People throughout this nation have received miracles, which they testify of today, because someone else thought enough of them to seek God on their behalf.

And when they were come to the multitude, there came to him a certain man, kneeling down to him, and saying, Lord, have mercy on my son: for he is a [lunatic], and sore vexed: for ofttimes he falleth into the fire, and oft into the water. And I brought him to thy disciples, and they could not cure him. Then Jesus answered and said, 'O faithless and perverse generation, how long shall I be with you? How long shall I suffer you? Bring him hither to me.' And Jesus rebuked the devil and he departed out of him: and the child was cured from that very hour. Then came the disciples to Jesus apart, and said, Why could not we cast him out? And Jesus said unto them, 'Because of your unbelief: for verily I say unto you, If ye have faith as a grain of mustard seed, ye shall say unto this mountain,

Remove hence to yonder place: and it shall remove; and nothing shall be impossible unto you. Howbeit this king goeth not out but by prayer and fasting.' (Matt. 17:14-21)

The disciples had their opportunity to make a difference in this young's man life, but they let it slip away. Now I know most persons that have preached sermons in reference to this boy being loosed from that demonic spirit, have striven on the disciples' lack of faith. It is true Jesus told them that because of their unbelief, they could not set him free; however there was still an important element missing. If we read verse twenty-one, we will note that Jesus told them, this particular miracle was not only going to take faith, but would require fasting and prayer. If more Christians would be willing to say no to food, for an extended period of time, while seeking the face of God, there would be no miracle that could not be wrought. Conversely, the situation today is that there are not many willing to put up this kind sacrifice for anyone else.

Now, other things occurred after this, which I found quite interesting. If we examine Luke's account of this situation, we find that after Jesus rebuked the unclean spirit, He healed the child, and delivered him back to his father. It is apparent that the father had gotten tired of not knowing how to deal with that spirit. The interesting aspect of this story is that the father knew the chain of command in leadership. He obviously thought that if he needed to bring his child anywhere for help, it should at least be the church. When he came, he did not go to the pastor of the church (Jesus), but he went to those who followed and were trained by Jesus. Therefore, lay members do not always have to run to the pastor with their problems, but there should be qualified assistants that can help the members with their situations. However, what good does training do if when it is time to exercise the training, you cannot deliver?

This man must have felt that Jesus was already under enough pressure, and that the disciples could cast the Devil out. Oftentimes we do not realize that when people go to the church that they are silently asking for help. People deal with issues from their jobs, marriages, finances, demonic activity dealing with their spirits to send them back into the world, and other things too numerous to mention, all week long. When they come to church, they are really saying, 'I believe this hospital has a physician in the house, please heal me!' When their healings and deliverance does not occur, they leave feeling empty or worse than when they came.

The disciples were not prepared to heal the child at that time. This may have been because they were caught up in their popularity, or excited to be chosen by Jesus. Whatever the case, they were not prepared to get the job done. When an opportunity presents itself, we must always be ready, and not turn it down. Know that there will be some, who will come to the church without good intentions, and who will allow the enemy to use them to stir up trouble. These people the Lord will drive out in due season, thus, the pastor won't even need to worry about the aims of these trouble-makers because they will not prosper.

Then there are those that will come hurting and looking for answers like this man. He was not just among the lay members in a crowd, but he had purpose. He obviously endeavored to build his trust in the church, but went to those that were not in position at the appropriate time. Thus, the man had to bother Jesus to cast that spirit out of the boy.

Jesus found out quickly where the hearts of His disciples were, after He revealed His identity to them, saying, **"…for the Son of man shall be delivered into the hands of men" (Luke 9:44-46).** When He spoke these words, the disciples started debating and arguing over who would be the greatest or become the leader. You see, their priorities were not in order. The disciples should have been seeking to be in their

rightful place, not the place in which they wanted to see themselves. Many folks desire to see themselves doing great exploits, but they do not want to seek the face of God for right standing with Him.

"And John answered and said, Master, we saw one casting out devils in thy name; and we forbade him, because he followeth not with us." (Luke 9:49)

Observe what happens when we are not seeking God, as we ought to, we find fault with others. Because of their deficiency, the disciples saw someone, who was not in their church, being using Jesus's name and being effective, and became jealous. All of the disciples together could not cast out **a demon**, but when they saw one man casting out **demons**, they told him to stop. The disciples felt embarrassed because, up until this point, they had been caught up in pride, conceit or arrogance. This must have been the case otherwise why would they have wanted to stop the man from casting out demons?

Many Christians are on an ego trip, and when they fail where someone else succeeds, they feel inadequate. I find that when a person is in their rightful position they do not have to be jealous over anyone else's accomplishments, but rather, they celebrate with them. Just because someone is not a part of your church, organization, social club, group or clique, does not mean that they are not on the Lord's side. There are people, who when you fast and pray, will think you are trying to act overly spiritual or deep, but do not allow their opinion of you to stop you from seeking God or doing God's will. Jesus, told John, 'don't stop him! Anyone, who is not against you, is for you.' (see Luke 9:50)

Daniel Made a Difference

Darius, the king, decided to divide his kingdom into 120 provinces, and after doing so, he appointed twenty princes to rule the provinces of the kingdom. Darius was a man that needed other people around him for his company to run smoothly. If he had to do most of the thinking himself, he probably would have failed as the king. King Darius also appointed three presidents of which Daniel, a wise man, was the leader. Thus, Daniel was over the twenty princes and two presidents that were going to rule Darius's kingdom. Daniel found favor above all of the princes and presidents, due to his excellent spirit and his abilities. I do not want you to think that Daniel was a Christian, who let his light shine, but was inadequate at getting his job done. There are many Christians today that flop at jobs, but they will praise the Lord wherever they go. Praising the Lord on your job does not cover up for your laziness, unethical behaviors, or inabilities to perform the job. Stop hiding behind Christianity and either get a job, or hold onto the one you have. God did not call for every person, who is a Christian, to give up his/her job to go into the ministry full-time. The only full-time persons should be the pastor and essential staff members, if the ministry has grown to the point where it can support these individuals. So please do not quit your job, and say, 'God told me to go into the ministry full time,' unless He truly has. If the Lord really did not tell you to go full-time, you will be right back in the market looking for a job before the year is up. Although Daniel was a God fearing man, he too realized that he had to work to support himself.

Although Daniel worked under extreme difficulty with those who did not believe in God, he worked more efficiently than with the other administrators. Daniel never sat around waiting for someone to do his job for him. He proved to be a quality employee, which attracted the attention of his boss, the king. King Darius thought within himself to place Daniel over the entire kingdom. However, the other two administrators and princes sought to find fault with Daniel. They tried there level best to find problems with how Daniel performed his job, but they found none.

We can clearly see how easy it is to make enemies just by doing the job you are hired to do. As you produce results, someone will be watching, and thinking, 'you must think you are all that!' There will always be faultfinders, looking for a reason to criticize your work. The easiest way to handle your critics is to live a godly life at all times. Do not conform to their ways one day, and the next day not speak to them. If you live a life above reproach, you will find your enemies will have no negative influence against you. There will be times when you will be criticized, and will be hurt, but realize that your helper is on the way. There are three things, which will always work in your favor, if you maintain your Christian walk:

- ✞ God will move your enemies out of your way
- ✞ God will give you a better opportunity elsewhere
- ✞ God will make you the boss, and you will set the standard.

The presidents and the princes came to realize Daniel was faithful, reliable, and a man of integrity. They concluded, 'we will not be able to find fault in him, except we find it against the law of his God.' If the only fault someone can find with you is your belief, count it all joy that it is your belief in God and not something you have done to disgrace the kingdom of God. Normally, when people have to attack your belief, it is because they really do not have anything else to negatively comment about, which is a good thing.

<u>How do you respond to such behavior?</u>

(1) Never stop believing in God,

(2) Do not compromise to get along with anyone, and

(3) Stay humble through it all, the Lord will fight your battles.

I hope you now realize that it is easy for people in the world to come together, when they are all in the wrong. None of these men had a relationship with God except Daniel, thus they came together to conspire against him. All of the presidents, governors, princes, advisors, and officials went to the king and told him they had unanimously agreed that if any man would pray to any other God, except the king, he should be cast into a den of lions. They sought the approval of the king on this matter, and he gladly agreed. An individual, who cannot make decisions on his own, is not a good leader. Leaders are innovators, not copy artists, and they set the standard, they do not accept the standard of others. King Darius signed the decree into law, and from that point onward, it had to be enforced.

King Darius was an effective king, but he was weak to the counsel of others, because when making decisions, he did not count up the costs for himself. Most leaders have advisors, but your advisors should not make your decisions for you, if you can think for yourself. The Devil will also send people in your midst to try to destroy the plan of God, and normally it happens through those that are close to you, such as through your advisors. From the time these men walked into his court with this foolishness, he could have asked them if they were out of their minds to even suggest such a thing, but he entertained them.

Daniel very well knew of the signing of the law and what it constituted, but he did not sway one bit. He still kept his daily regiment of prayer, praying three times a day even with his windows opened. Daniel proved he would not conform to their law just to keep his job, and that he was not ashamed of his belief in God. It is so easy for a child of God to get off track while they are in school, on the job, or even around some friends. It can only happen though, if you are not sold out to the kingdom. Daniel was a consecrated man, who was disciplined and had his mind focused on God. He never tried to fit in the clique to make friends, or compromise his standards for a job. We make too excuses for the disruption of our prayer life. Some allow their jobs, social activities, and just plain idleness, to keep them away from seeking God. Constant prayer and fasting, however, will keep your line of communication open with God. Thus, when trouble should arise, your prayer will already be answered.

The officials knew that at certain times of the day, Daniel would be in devotion. Therefore, they went to his home at this time, and found him praying and seeking God for direction. Just as people that are corrupt, who want to see you fall as well, the officials went to the king immediately. They asked the king, isn't it true you have signed a decree, **"that every man that shall ask a petition of any god or man within thirty days, [except] you, O king, shall be cast into the den of lions?"** The king answered and said, **"the thing is true, according to the law of the Medes and Persians, which altereth not" (Daniel 6:12).**

In Babylon, the king's word was the law. In Medo-Persia, when a law was made not even the king could change it. These men related to the king the fact that Daniel was in his house, not paying heed to the king's law, but still praying three times a day to his God. The way in which the presidents and princes related this message to the king, angered King Darius. He was angry because although he really wanted to spare Daniel, not even he could overturn his own law. Thus, the king spent the rest of the day looking for a way to get Daniel out of this situation. Nonetheless, Daniel's accusers reminded the king that even he could not change the law. Finally, the king gave the order to arrest Daniel and have him thrown into the lions' den.

At that time, lions would roam about the countryside in the forests of Mesopotamia. The people feared them greatly, and respected what they could do to them. The Persians would also capture lions, feed them, and use them for execution purposes. Regardless, Daniel's attitude as he was escorted to the lions' den was no different than before. Once inside of the den, a stone was placed at the mouth of the den, to secure it so that no one could rescue Daniel. The king told him, **"Daniel, thy God you serve continually, he will deliver thee"(Daniel**

6:16). The king went to his palace that night and fasted. He refused to listen to any music, and did not sleep all night.

Very early the next morning the king rushed to the lions' den. He cried out ***"Daniel, servant of the living God, is thy God, whom thou servest continually, able to deliver thee from the lions?" (Daniel 6:20).*** Daniel answered, 'Long live the king! My God sent his angels that they shut the mouths so that they would not hurt me, for I have been found innocent in His sight. And I have not wronged you, Your Majesty.' The king was so overwhelmed that he ordered Daniel out of the den. Then the king gave orders to arrest the men who accused Daniel. He had them thrown in the lions' den, along with their wives, and children. Before they could even hit the floor of the den, the lions leaped on them, and tore them apart.

It never pays to do anyone evil, because it hurts much more when it comes back to you. People that even plan evil for others should realize that their plan could easily backfire on them.

Daniel made a difference by his continuous fasting and prayerful life. As a result of Daniel's faith towards God, the king decreed unto all of the nation that ***"in every dominion of [his] kingdom that men tremble and fear the God of Daniel: For he is the living God, and steadfast forever, and his kingdom shall not be destroyed, and his dominion shall be even to the end" (Daniel 6:26).*** If Daniel made that kind of stand in his day, shouldn't we be able to make just as great a difference today.

The Kingdom is Restored

When the disciples came into the ministry of apostles, they asked Jesus, ***"Lord wilt thou at this time restore again the kingdom to Israel? And he said unto them, 'It is not for you to know the times or the season, which the Father hath put in his own power. But ye*** *shall receive power, after that the Holy Ghost is come upon you, and ye shall be witnesses unto me both in Jerusalem, and in all Judaea, and in Samaria, and unto the uttermost part of the earth" (Acts 1:6-8)*

Every avid Bible student knows that the Apostles began to seek for the baptism of the Holy Ghost. They all came together, including Mary the mother of Jesus, and went into serious seeking. Fifty days after the resurrection, and ten days after the ascension, the Holy Ghost came and filled all of the believers who did not stop seeking for it. Do you want to know what can you do to receive it? You can start seeking for the power right now. You do not have to fall into the same rut that so many powerless preachers fall into. Some are still striving off their father's anointing and others are preaching out of obligation because they come from a line of preachers. No, that is not the way nor the reason to preach. The way is to push that dinner plate aside and deny your flesh, to feed the spirit. The Apostles received because they realized they could not ride off Jesus's anointing, they had to get it for themselves.

You can make a difference by becoming completely serious about what God has called you to do!

And when he had called unto him his twelve disciples, he gave them power against unclean spirits, to cast them out, and to heal all manner of sickness and all manner of disease...These twelve Jesus sent forth, and commanded them, saying, 'Go not into the way of the Gentiles, and into any city of the Samaritans enter ye not: But go rather to the lost sheep of the house of Israel. And as ye go, preach, saying, The kingdom of heaven is at hand. Heal the sick, cleanse the lepers, raise the dead, cast out devils: freely ye have received, freely give'. (Matt. 10:1,5-8)

This is what you can do to make a difference, but it will take the true power of God. You cannot get this kind of power by sitting back and waiting for it to come, by reading a Bible story, or because you saw someone else with it. In order to have it, you must seek for it with your whole heart.

On many occasions, people went to hear Jesus preach as they knew the word would be backed by following signs because of His anointing. Today some people go to church because they want someone to motivate them and tell them how everything is going to be alright. Inwardly they are still broken, confused, and disgusted with themselves and those around them.

Jesus was so anointed that He challenged sickness and disease. He went down to Simon Peter's home, and his mother-in-law was sick in bed with a high fever. Immediately, they told Jesus of her illness, and Jesus went to her bedside, took her by the hand, lifted her up, and immediately the fever left. The woman got up and starting cooking dinner for Jesus and her family (See Mark 1:29-31)

Several days later Jesus returned to Capernaum, and the word had gotten out that He was in town. The people ran to the house where He was staying, and packed the house out, whereas there was not even enough for anyone else to enter, nor was there space outside of the door. Nonetheless, the first thing Jesus did was to preach unto the people. When the word is preached with power, lives will be changed forever. As a result, these people could not keep their deliverance to themselves, but went out and spread the word to others. It is a selfish thing when people say they want to make a difference, but they are afraid to tell others about the goodness of God and what He is capable of doing. God does not need people to hold back on the gospel, He needs those that will be willing to seek Him and boldly go into the highways and hedges and to compel others to come.

When Paul spoke to the Corinthian church, he stated to the brethren that when he came to them he did not come with excellency of speech or of wisdom, but rather, he declared unto them the testimony of God.

He was determined not to know anything about them except that which related to Jesus Christ. (See I Cor. 2:1-2).

Similarly, Paul told the church at Thessalonica, *"For our gospel came not unto you in word only, but also in power, and in the Holy Ghost, and in much assurance, as ye know what manner of men we were among you for your sake. And ye became followers of us, and of the lord, having received the word in much affliction, with joy of the Holy Ghost."(I Thess. 1:5- 6)*

As we can clearly see, the apostle had power, and he demonstrated it. Paul was not a man that spoke about miracles, he had miracle working power working on his life. This man, who was chief among sinners, became one of the greatest apostles to live. After his conversion, Paul immediately began preaching, that Jesus Christ was the Son of God, in the synagogues.

Paul obeyed the Lord and when he first began preaching, he ministered to the Jews. Some Jews fostered theological arguments against Paul and Barnabas. However, on the following Sabbath day, almost the entire city came to hear the word of God. When the Jews that did not receive Paul, saw the multitude of Gentiles getting excited about the word, they were filled with jealousy. Luke pointed out why they had a problem seeing the people accept the word Paul and Barnabas preached unto them, they were envious. These Jews were not making a difference in the lives of the Gentiles, and after witnessing the response from the people, they were completely upset.

Sometimes when we see other persons abiding in their calling and making the most of it, we get jealous because we are not succeeding as we should. It is hard for some people to rejoice with others when they break new ground, if they have not been able to. Getting jealous is the reaction of many of Christians, yet they will never acknowledge it. It is a terrible thing when people become so jealous that they try to hinder the work of God.

Every word that Paul spoke, these Jews disputed. Paul's response was that it was necessary that the word be preached unto them first, but seeing that they rejected the word, he and the other disciples offered it to the Gentiles. Paul was telling the Jews that he had indeed done his part as the Lord commanded them, but they did not want to accept the word (See Acts 13).

There was a time when this same man did not make a positive difference, but persecuted the church. He had favor with the Chief Priests, so they encouraged his actions. Later on however, the same persons that encouraged his motives were the ones who destroyed him. When you work for the Devil, it will not be long before he turns on you. Jews came from Antioch, and Iconium to stone Paul, however, they thought they killed him, but he got away. When you are making a difference, the Devil will do whatever he can to destroy you. He will try with lies, scandals, backbiting, and hypocrisy from those you believe are on your side.

There was a time that the apostles made a difference through the multitude of signs and wonders they wrought. Believers were added to the church, insomuch that the sick were brought in beds and couches to the church. As Peter passed, people would receive miracles. Sick folks were healed and demons fled, due to the consecrated lives of these men. People came from all over to receive the word and their miracle.

Thus, the High Priest called the council together to figure out what to do with the apostles, because nothing they tried had succeeded. The apostles were even jailed, but an angel of the Lord came and opened up the gates to the jail, then sent them back out into the streets to start preaching again. Those that God has truly called are not going to fit in with cliques, but their goal will be to please God. There is little talk today about men and women of God being cast out because they preach or tell the truth. If you compromise the word of God for people, you will become an enemy with God.

While the apostles were preaching, the High Priest arrived and sent for them to be taken out of jail, and brought before the council. What he did not know was that the Lord had set them free to start preaching again, because they were making a difference. The apostles did not sit around wondering what their next move would be, but rather, they obeyed the voice of God. If more people that claim to hear from God, would learn to be obedient, they would grow a whole lot faster. The captain of the temple guard went along with the leading priests and arrested the apostles, asking, "did not we command you not to teach or preach in the name of Jesus?" Peter told them, we much rather obey God than man.

When the Lord has called you to make a difference, do not sit around waiting on people to do it for you; otherwise, it will never be done. The high council was furious and wanted to destroy the apostles, but one man had a different perspective about the entire matter. This man was Gamaliel, a man extremely knowledgeable about the law. He told his constituents to leave the men alone. He reasoned that if the work the apostles were doing be of men, it would come to nothing, but if it be of God, they would not be able to stop them. Gamaliel also warned them that if they interfered, they might also have to deal with God Himself (See Acts 5).

If the Lord has chosen for you to make a difference, regardless of what happens, your work will be fulfilled. No one will be able to stand in your way, despite what they may do, and you will be unstoppable unless you stop yourself.

Apostle. Dr. P.W. Reed, Ph.D.

Chapter - 11

Not Without a Fight

The True Apostolic Anointing

I think it is important for me to note what an apostle is. The word *"apostle"* in Greek terminology is *"apostolos"* which means a delegate; an ambassador of the Gospel; officially, a commissioner of Christ (one who operates in miraculous power).

In common language, we have noted that apostles are those that establish churches and ministries up from the ground floor to a thriving ministry. A true apostle's ministry is not limited to national boundaries, but is international, to which missions outreach is a part of his ministry. An apostle is one that not only starts a local church, but has bishops, overseers, pastors, and ministers under his covering or umbrella.

More importantly than Webster's or man's definitions, an apostle is one that has paid a price, and will continue to pay a price for his anointing. The Devil hates true apostles because they stand for everything Jesus stood for. Anyone, that establishes churches where the power of God resides and where demons are trembling, will be a threat to the enemy. True apostles endure the storm, rain, scandals, and rumors that the normal pastor may not have to go through. Even more, they have a past that can relate to almost any situation because they have gotten experience through trial and error.

And they said unto him, Why do the disciples of John fast often, and make prayers, and likewise the disciples of the Pharisees; but thine eat and drink: And he said unto them, Can ye make the children of the bridechamber fast, while the bridegroom is with them? But the days will come, when the bridegroom shall be taken away from them, and then shall they fast in those days. (Luke 5:33-35)

When the religious leaders complained to Jesus about the fact that His disciples were feasting instead of fasting at a wedding celebration, He asked them if wedding guests usually fasted while they celebrated with the groom. He continued to say that the day would come when the groom would not be around and at that time, they would fast. Jesus's point was that when He left in bodily form, the disciples, who later became apostles, would have to fast.

In Acts 1, Jesus showed Himself to the apostles for forty days, and He spoke of things pertaining to the kingdom. He taught them many things regarding staying in relationship with Him, although He would not be with them in bodily form. Jesus also informed them, that although (in Matthew 10) He had given them power against unclean spirits to cast them out, (gr. *Exousia*- ability, privilege, jurisdiction, liberty), they would still need to seek God for the power to go to the next level (gr. *Dunamis*-miraculous power, abundant ability, mighty works). Thus, we can clearly see that there is a distinction between the two powers. The first, *Exousia*, is the ability or liberty granted by God for a specific purpose. A person that operates in *Exousia*, does not have to seek for it. Mind you, however, *Dunamis* comes as a result of a person seeking for it on his own. The apostles did not just wait for the power to fall upon them, they acted, because they wanted this power inside of them and operating on the outside. *Dunamis* comes through much fasting and prayer; in other words, there is a price to pay for this kind of power.

I believe that if we are going to get a clear understanding of a true apostle, not one self appointed –who starts a church and is not acknowledged among his constituents as an apostle -but a man of God who has paid a price, we should measure his life according to the life of the Apostle Paul. Apostle Paul, before he became an apostle, was known as Saul. According to Acts 9, Saul uttered threats against the Christians with every breath he had. He requested letters from the high priest to address the synagogues in Damascus, asking cooperation to arrest any follower of Christ. His desire was to bring them from Damascus down to Jerusalem in chains. As he neared Damascus, however, he was blinded by a bright light shining from heaven, causing him to fall to the ground. Saul fell saying, "who art you Lord?" The Lord replied, "I am Jesus who thou persecutest," it is hard for you to fight against me. From that point on Paul received his ministry. He was anointed by a man of God, Ananias, and through Ananias's hand, Saul's eyes became open. Then he was baptized and received the Holy Ghost. Immediately, Paul started preaching the gospel in synagogues, and in Jerusalem.

But Saul increased the more in strength and confounded the Jews which dwelt at Damascus, proving that this is very Christ… Then Saul, (who also is called Paul,) filled with the Holy Ghost, set his eyes on him, and said, O full of all subtly and all mischief, thou child of the devil, thou enemy of the all righteousness, wilt thou not cease to pervert the right ways of the Lord. (Acts 9:22; 13:9-10)

We can clearly see that Saul's name and his behavior had changed, as he was completely converted.

Paul preached in Paphos, Perga, Pamphylia, and Antioch in many synagogues, and later established churches all over Rome, Ephesus,

Corinth, Galatia and in other places. He became a true apostle, not by appointment, but by anointing.

An apostle is chosen by God, not by man. As seen in I Corinthians 1:1, Paul was *"called to be an Apostle of Jesus Christ through the will of God, and Sosthenes our brother."*

He contined to say, *"Am I not an apostle? Am I not free? Have I not seen Jesus Christ our Lord? Are not ye my work in the Lord? If I be not an apostle unto others, yet doubtless I am to you: for the zeal of mine apostleship are ye in the Lord…For I am least of the apostles, that am not meet to be called an apostle, because I persecuted the church of God. But by the grace of God I am what I am: and his grace which was bestowed upon me was not in vain; but I labored more abundantly than they all: yet not I, but the grace of God which was with me. Therefore whether it were I or they, so we preach, and so ye believed." (I Cor. 9:1-2; 15 9-11)*

"This is a faithful saying, and worthy of all acceptation, that Christ Jesus came into the world to save sinners; of whom I am chief." (I Tim. 1:15)

An Apostle has to be all things to all men. 'When in Rome, he does as the Romans do' because he knows how to adjust. He can go to Ethiopia and eat the food they eat, or fast, and will not be affected by his surroundings. He does not seek approval of men, nor does he worry about the opinions of others, because he knows that whatever he does is for the betterment of the kingdom of God. He is also builder and goes to places that some men would dare not go. He is free with himself and with God. True apostles also, do not seek to become apostles. Rather it happens without them even being aware of it, until God speaks to them and reveals to them that they are apostles.

All apostles, who have been appointed by God, have been to hell and back. They did not get where they are, because they chose to be there, but rather because God placed them there without any warning.

Most apostles have lost out on what appeared to be much (wealth), before God gave them that more in the end. The enemy has tried to make them loose their mind, marriages, families, security, reputations and everything connected to them. Satan is always angry with them because they impact nations, not just a few people.

In II Corinthians 11: 23-28, Paul describes the tribulations he had endured:

Are they ministers of Christ? (I speak as a fool) I am more; in labours more abundant, in stripes above measure, in prison more frequent, in deaths oft. Of the Jews five times received I forty stripes save one. Thrice was I beaten with rods, once was I stoned, thrice I suffered shipwreck, and night and a day I have been in the deep; In journeyings often, in perils of waters, in perils of robbers, in perils by mine own contrymen, in perils by the heathen, in perils in the city, in perils in the wilderness, in perils in the sea, in perils among false brethren; I weariness and painfulness, in watchings often, in hunger and thirst, in fastings often, in cold and nakedness. Beside those things that are without, that which cometh upon me daily, the care of all the churches.

For the true apostle, things get better, but they never become easier, because the fight from Satan's demons is always present. The enemy uses people, places, and things to fight an apostle both in the church and outside of the church. Satan's ultimate goal is to see the man of God sifted as wheat, to stop his purpose, and to see that all of the souls the apostle has helped to be saved, become lost. The enemy hates when this man of God fasts and prays, because he knows God will reveal something else new and fresh in his spirit for the next level. If you are a true apostle, you will have a fight from most everyone, even some that follow you in ministry. I truly believe that out of every twelve members someone in the church is going to let the enemy use them against you. Therefore, apostles be on guard of your Judas!

Apostle. Dr. P.W. Reed, Ph.D.

Chapter - 12

When a Man Knows to Do Good

"Therefore to him that knoweth to do good, and doeth it not, to him it is sin." (James 4:17)

Now the word of the Lord came unto Jonah the son of Amittai, saying, arise go to Nineveh, that great city and cry against it; for their wickedness is come up before me. But Jonah rose up to flee unto Tarshish from the presence of the Lord, and went down to Joppa; and he found a ship going to Tarshish; so he paid the fare thereof, and went down into it, to go with them unto Tarshish from the presence of the Lord. But the Lord sent out a great wind into the sea, and there was a mighty tempest in the sea, so that the ship was like to be broken. Then the mariners were afraid, and cried every man unto his god, and cast forth the wares that were in the ship into the sea, to lighten it of them. But Jonah was gone down into the sides of the ship; and he lay, and was fast asleep. So the shipmaster came to him, and said unto him, What meanest thou, O sleeper? Arise, call upon thy God, if so be that God will think upon us, that we perish not. (Jonah 1:1-6)

Now I know that there are people who are reluctant about moving at the word of God from a prophet, pastor, or evangelist, but we have to be so careful that when it is God speaking we are obedient, otherwise we can find ourselves out of the will of God. Examining the disobedience of Jonah will reveal this point.

Jonah was a prophet who prophesied during the reign of Jeroboam II, the king of Israel from 793 to 753 B.C. Jonah is mentioned in 2 Kings 14:25, so he could have been a member of that company of prophets. Now, God told Jonah to go to Ninevah and warn the people of soon coming judgement. Ninevah, the capital city of Assyria, was disobedient unto God in that they exploited the helpless, were idolatrous, and committed prostitution and witchcraft (Nahum 1,2,3,4). The people needed to repent to God, and if they did God would grant them mercy. In this case, Jonah had obviously heard from God Himself, not a man.

Jonah, however, had his own personal hatred against Ninevah and wanted to see them destroyed. He had no desire to allow the people to repent or see God show them mercy. So, just as Israel was selfish with God, and did not want to see non-Jews receive the favor of God, Jonah wanted to see the Ninevites punished. I find that in a many cases the thing we do not want to do, is the very thing that God will have us confront. Jonah needed to get delivered from the way he felt towards the Ninevites, because through him they would receive deliverance. In other words, in ministry there cannot be any kind of prejudice in our heart if we desire to be effective. Ministry is not for a certain kind of group or people; salvation is for everyone.

When God spoke to Jonah, He knew Ninevah was toward the east, and Tarshish west. The Lord does not need us to altar His plan for our lives, because the more you rebel the harder it will be for you. Sometimes we run in another direction when God is telling us to stand where we are, or do things His way. Stubborness, fear, selfishness, or rebellion can cause you to run in the opposite direction than the direction that God is calling for you to go. Anytime God tells a person to do something, it always turns out good. I do not care what you have to go through before you hit your destiny, it will still turn out positively. We know that *"all things work together for good to them that love God, to them who are the called according to his purpose"* (Rom 8:28). I find that no one that seeks the face of God is on the run. The only time we run, or cannot hear from God is when we are hiding something, or trying to hide from God.

In the process of God desiring to bring deliverance to Ninevah, God also needed to deliver Jonah from his prejudice views about those who were ungodly. All preachers should always remember that as we preach to others, we preach to ourselves first. That is why Apostle Paul said, *"I keep under my body and bring it into subjection; lest that by any means, when I have preached to others, I myself should be a castaway (I Cor. 9:27).* It is clear that when a person is in rebellion he cannot hear from anyone. Rebellious people get mad with the church and blame their cursed state on their local church. When members of the church try to call them, they avoid them by acting as if they are not home, leaving the answering service on. Some even go so far as to tell their kids to lie and say that they are not home. These people are on the run! If the flesh is not put under subjection, I don't care how anointed you think you are, or how well you preach, the Devil will cause you to run. Although you know to do what is right, you will not be able to hear from God and will do wrong. When we stop seeking God through fasting and prayer, we cannot hear from God; it is as though we are disconnected. Have you ever spoken to someone on the phone, and all of a udden the line goes dead, yet you kept speaking? Know matter how much you talk, the person on the other end will not hear you because he has lost communication with you. If a person loses their communication with God, they can know to do good, or to do the right thing, but yet they will not do it.

The Devil got great joy out of seeing Jonah running to Tarshish, because he knew Jonah was out of position. Jonah had become a castaway and fugitive on the run. He thought he was running from wicked people, but in fact he was running from God. The Bible says, ***"He therefore that despiseth, despiseth not man, but God, who hath also given unto us his holy spirit (1Thes. 4:8).*** Running put Jonah in a worse position. If he had not run several things he went through would not have happened.

The Lord sent out a great wind into the sea, and a mighty tempest arose breaking the ship (see Jonah 1:4).

Wherefore they cried unto the Lord, and said, We beseech thee, O Lord, we beseech thee, let us not perish for this man's life, and lay not upon us innocent blood: for thou, O Lord, hast done as it pleased thee. So they took up Jonah, and cast him forth into sea: and the sea ceased from her ragging. Then the men feared the Lord exceedingly, and offered a sacrifce unto the Lord, and made vows. Now the Lord had prepared a great fish to swallow up Jonah. And Jonah was in the belly of the fish three days and three nights. (Jonah 1:14-17)

Much of the trouble we get into with God does not have anything to do with Him, nor did the Devil, but we put ourselves in these vulnerable positions. When we are not in our place with God where we need to be, we are not the only persons affected by it. We affect our families, friends, church and everyone whose lives are touched by ours. Although Jonah knew the right thing to do, he was disobedient, and as a result the lives of those on the ship were affected, although they did not even know him. What I found to be fascinating was the fact that the crew of the ship did not know Jonah, and were unwilling to sacrifice there own life for Jonah. They tried everything as a solution to their situation and when they realized Jonah was probably the cause. The whole crew began to cry out to the Lord, 'don't let us perish because of this man.' When things start going sour in your church, in your home, on your job or even in your finances, do not look at any one else but yourself. Jonah had to be honest with himself, and say 'I am the problem, cast me overboard.' Repentance and being honest with yourself is what brings deliverance. If there are things you used to do, and you know worked well, do not stop doing them. Most persons that are successful will let you know one of the keys to success is doing what it takes to become successful, over, and over again without changing anything.

The entire crew made a vow to serve God, and sacrificed unto Him, because they wanted deliverance. God always knows how to take a bad situation and still get glory out of it. Jonah had lost his prayer life, and did not feel an urge to seek the face of God. At one point the shipmaster came to Jonah and said, 'Man, everyone is calling on your god, and here you are down here sleeping!' *"Arise, and call upon thy God, if so be that God will think upon us, that we perish not" (Jonah 1:6).* Jonah knew he needed to pray, but it was not a reality to him that he needed to change at that point, so that other lives would not be affected. Thus, God had to prepare something that seemed negative to get Jonah back in his place. He sent a great fish to swallow Jonah up, and left him in the fish's belly for three days and three nights. I believe God had Jonah there to complete His purpose for his life. Jonah did not pray until he was in the belly of the fish, where he cried out unto the Lord.

Jonah said, *" 'When my soul fainted within me I remembered the Lord: and my prayer came in unto thee, into thine holy temple. They that observe lying vainities forsake their own mercy. But I will sacrifice unto thee with the voice of thanksgiving; I will pay that that I have vowed. Salvation is of the Lord.' And the Lord spake unto the fish, and it vomitted out Jonah upon the dry land" (Jonah 1:7-9).*

After Jonah repented and made a vow to God, the fish vomitted him out of his belly. *"Now Nineveh was an exceeding great city of three days' journey. And Jonah began to enter the city a day's journey, and he cried, and said, Yet forty days, and Ninevah shall be*

overthrown"(Jonah 3:3-4). Jonah ran so fast that he reached Ninevah in one day, even though it should have taken three. This shows you what can happen when a person is obedient. They will make great leaps and exploits faster than they would have even imagined.

God Spoke To Me!

The Lord spoke to me approximately eighteen years ago about moving to Boston, MA. to start another branch of Total Deliverance Ministries. However, I wanted to go to Atlanta, Ga. to live and start another church. I had a job offer at a local college and was so excited because I thought that this was my release to move to Atlanta. I had a brother that had already been living in Boston, that I had visited on two occasions, who asked me if would I consider living in Boston. I told him I would not dare live in Boston. Nonetheless, when I was on my way home from my interview with a college in Atlanta, I just happened to fall asleep behind the wheel of the car. My car flipped three times and landed on its tires; however, I thought I was dreaming. When the car stopped flipping, the Lord said, "I told you Boston!" It was now up to me to be obedient. There were college kids that came and helped me out of the ditch, asking me if I was married. I told them I was, and sent them to call my wife. She became frantic when she got the news, but they told her I was okay. Then I called my wife from Alabama, where the accident happened, and told her that the Lord said Boston. She told me, "if that was what God told you I'll start packing and we'll go."

At this particular time, I had been fasting and praying much for the will of God for my life, and my next move in ministry. My wife, daughter and I was on my way to Boston, on a cold winter day and as we approached New York City, the weather was so bad we could hardly see. By the time we got to Worcester, MA., my car jack-knifed into a heap of snow and was stuck with the front end in the air, and the rear end on the ground. I asked a gentleman to help me pull my car out of the snow as he pumped gas (he was pumping as quickly as possible to get out of that blizzard of snow). The man told me he would not help me because it was cold, and I must have been crazy. He said "I'm out of here!"

He left, and I cried. At that moment my wife asked me "what are we going to do?" My four year old daughter said, "Daddy we're going to be alright," and I said to my family, "let's pray someone is going to help us." We prayed, and my wife said, "now I know we are supposed to be in Boston, because the Devil is trying to stop us from getting there." I agreed, and after we had finished praying the same man that told me he would not help us, came back, put a chain on my car, and pulled me out of the snowbank. About an hour and a half later, I was in the Boston area.

Don't Let Anything Stop You !

I ran revivals in the city of Boston at several churches, and some asked me to join up with them, but I declined. I told them God had given me a vision for a church in the Boston area, and would soon start it when He released me. There was one gentleman, who every time he heard that I was going to be preaching at a church, would show up. One day I asked him, how he found out where I would be preaching at and he told me, "word gets around." Then he asked me if would I start a church and I replied "yes, when the Lord releases me." After that, he would call me everyday, and ask, "did the Lord speak to you yet?" After several of these calls, I told him the Lord told me at the end of January the church would start. I now had to find a building to get started in.

I was refused at every place I could find in the yellow pages, or wherever I saw a "FOR RENT" sign. All of the places with space to rent that I called, told me, "no"or "we cannot rent to churches for insurance reasons." Meanwhile, this man kept calling me daily, asking me if I had found a building yet, to which I would reply no. Soon, the first week of the month of January came. The following week I met another lady, who had heard me preach on more than one occasion, and asked if I was going to start a church. She explained her situation to me saying, "the place that I'm going to, I'm not growing and if you start a church I will be right there with my family." I told her the Lord had told me the church would open at the end of the month. So now if this did not happen I would look like a lying prophet. Obviously time was winding up, and the pressure was on. The Devil wanted me to stop believing God, and he tried his level best to discourage me.

Well, I got good news at the end of the second week: I found a building. The building was in a small district of Boston called Mattapan. My now only friend in Boston called me again, asking if I had found a building, to which I said yes! Oh, boy was I excited. When I told him it was in Mattapan, he replied, "I thought you told me the Lord told you Hyde Park, MA." I told him that yes he was right, but I could not find a building anywhere else. He said, "if God said Hyde Park, He will provide." Of course you do not have to read between the lines to know that I was upset with him, and did not want him calling my house any more. Nevertheless, I told him, "you are right, God said Hyde Park." Regardless, I knew that I wanted to be in the will of God, and because I did not want my car flipping again, I quickly agreed.

I found a building in Hyde Park to have worship service, by looking in the phone book one more time. It was a V.F.W. hall, but nontheless I called and asked them if they would rent their building for church services. The gentleman on the phone told me yes. Enough said, I drove to the building the same day, and sealed the deal. On the Sunday, January 21, 1995, we were having our very first church service. The same gentleman that I had stayed in contact with attended the service with his family, along with the lady I spoke with on the street and her children. Today, that gentleman is the head of my deacon board, and the lady is my personal secretary as well as the Head Deaconess,

Sunday school teacher, and an active member of my Pastoral Care Ministry.

It's Not Supposed to Be Easy; It's a Challenge!

The first year, approximately 125 new souls were added to the body of Christ in our church, and we were forced to move to a larger building. During this time tour ministry had a fight from people that were not a part of our church. Preachers would talk about me in their messages, although directly not using my name, but saying we stole their members, and that these little young preachers (like me) did not want to sit under anyone. Yet, we used a sister's house for our prayer nights, and kept fasting through it all.

By the second year we had our own building to worship in, so we started overnight prayer meetings, and shut-ins. The second year did not get easier, however, as some of the members started acting up, and making things more difficult than they needed to be. The church that I pastored, was nontheless determined to continue to fast. In our third year, we completed seven straight day fasts, as well as three and four day fasts, without anything to drink except water. In our fourth year, the Devil was so heated because we had fasted and prayed so often, that he was determinded to destroy God's house. Nonetheless, his plans did not prosper. The fifth year we went on a fourteen day fast, and shut-in. Most people only left the church to go to work, and then in the evening would come back to the church, and stay all night long. Now if you know anything about fasting, you know that God always blesses, but the enemy is still busy.

The Devil came after I chastised someone at her mother's request, because the child had been disobedient, and had being smoking mariuana. The young lady had also gotten into a fight with three people, who beat her up. This young lady looked up to me, and thought of me as a father. At the time, her aunt had been a member of our church, but when a situation did not go the way the aunt wanted for it to go, she got upset with me and left the church. When she left, I knew she was angry with me, but I did not think she was angry enough to try to hurt me. She was! This woman persuaded the young lady to lie and say I bruised her body. Low and behold, the police came and arrested me, then threw me in jail. Our church, however, came together that evening and, as was always taught, prayed.

Always know, but do not be afraid that when you fast the way God desires, the Devil will get busy. During the time of the trial, I was completing a fourteen day fast. The day I had to stand before the judge, I was asked whether I wanted to plead guilty, and go to jail for thirty days or go to trial. I am a firm believer, that if you are not guilty of something, never settle out of court. I said, "let's go to trial." The day my trial began, the people in the church had to erect the tent for our "Azusa Tent Revival" that was going to start the same night, by themselves. I told them that I would see them later, when I preached.

At the trial when it was time for the plaintiffs to testify, the judge and the jurors could decipher that they had their own personal issues with me, and had conjured up lies. The jurors deliberated and came back after lunch. While the judge was speaking to them asking them what their verdict was, they exclaimed, "Not Guilty."

After that my wife ministered to me and told me that I was too nice to people and should stop trying to help everyone. I explained to her that I am an Overseer and my job is to help people. Then I told her to stop being so crictical. My wife has always been protective of me, and watches those that I allow to get around me, because men, sometimes regardless of how spiritual we are, we still do not see everything the Devil sets up for us.

In the fifth year of the church in Boston, my family and I allowed someone to come and live in our home. This person's family had been going through financial diffiulties, and the child needed somewhere to stay. We tried to be nice again, escpecially me. I said, "let the child come stay with us," and I became her legal guardian. I find that you have to watch every spirit that you allow to come into your home. After all of the years I had been taught to fast and pray, now I found I could not fast as I used to. My wife and I started arguing a lot. I did not want to admit that it was because I let a child in my home. My wife said, "she has to go," but I said, "no, she's a child." The church people thought my wife was just being mean, but she was not being mean, she just wanted the spirit that was causing confusion out of her house. So the devil attacked our home heavily and destroyed what we had worked to build.

That Spirit Wants Your Home

Satan had me under his control, and I did not even know it. I was trying to be nice to someone, but I did not realize the Devil was trying to kill me in the long run. My wife was under a great deal of pressure, and my daughter felt as though I had been sharing her attention with someone else, which I was. I spent countless nights casting demons out of the child, which had had her bound for years. That spirit had entered my home and did not want to leave. Every time my wife would say, "she has to go," I would say, "no, she's a child." One thing we must know is that the Devil is no child; he has been around for a long time and the only thing that has change about him is his name. He was Lucifer, and now he is Satan, but all in all he is still the Devil and he wants your home. Later, the same family I tried to help, turned on me, and tried to have me lose my family, my home, my ministry and all of the things I had worked so hard to achieve.

I tried to fast through it, but I could only fast for one or two days a week, sporadically. Even after that spirit left my home, it still tried to follow me. I found that the enemy had me loosing my memory, forgetting things that I would normally not have forgotten, and saying things that I knew were not normal for me to say.

I started a church in New Orleans, and my wife went there to Pastor it. Rumors then begin that we were getting a divorce and that had I sent her there because we were not together. I told my wife I would try to be home at least every other week. That plan did not work for too long as my returns to New Orleans changed to once a month. Our relationship had changed tremendously, and the enemy had us as if we strangers to one another. I purchased a big house in New Orleans, but yet, it was not a home, because my family was not together.

When The Lord Speaks

I was in prayer in New Orleans, LA., and asked the Lord what was it that He wanted from me. I felt alone, as if everyone was against me. Each time I tried to help someone, I appeared as a bad person. The Lord spoke to me three weeks later, while I cried before Him, and told me, "you have prophesied to nations of people and yet will I not speak to you!" Then the Lord said, "I'm going to tell you what I want you to do, and don't question it." He left, and I went on a two day fast, neither eating nor drinking. I thought the Lord would not come back to me, but He did days later, and asked me, "do you love me?" I replied, "yes Lord." He asked again, "Reed do you love me?" I said, "yes, Lord." The Lord came back days later and asked again, "DO YOU LOVE ME?" I said, "yes!" Then He commanded me to:

1. Find a pastor for the New Orleans Church, you will know who he is.
2. Sell your house in New Orleans.
3. Move back to Boston with your family, for a house divided against itself cannot stand.

Of course when the Lord spoke these three things, I was in awe. I was not stupid enough to question God, though. I thought within myself, 'who will I get to pastor this church? Also, I just bought this house a year ago, now I have to sell it, move back to Boston full time, with my family? They don't even like Boston!' The Lord knew my thoughts and told me, "I have a pastor for this church, I will sell your home at the right time, and start enjoying being in Boston and in due season I'll move you if you faint not." I said yes, Lord and decided not to look back. I knew God had spoken to me and as a result I immediately felt as if I was back in spiritual control; God was talking to me again. I realized He had never left, but the enemy was trying to blind me. After this, I was concencrated to the office of Apostle/Bishop Prelate over Total Deliverance Ministries Family Worship Center.

Today, I am a Bishop/ Apostle and have connected churches in South Africa, Trinidad, New Orleans, and Boston, MA., and now in Atlanta, GA. My home in New Orleans has just been sold, and that same week, I started the paper work on an almost new home in the Boston area. The Lord commanded that the church and I to go on a thirty day fast before our Holy Convocation. Today, my current family and I are extremely happy about what God has done.

911- A State Of Emergency

You may be wondering why I subtitled the last part of my book "911." The reason is that it is September 11, 2001, the last few minutes before my birthday. What does that have to do with 911? Well, as I think about the last 20 minutes in which I will be the age that I am currently, I realize that time is running out for me to meet my deadline of completing this book before 12:00 A.M. My goal was to complete this book before that happened.

There is a more important reason, though. It is because God has let me know that we are truly living in the last days. On this day, early in the morning at approximately 8:14 A.M. there was a terriost take-over on a 767 Jet leaving Boston, the city where I live, to Los Angeles, CA. That plane never made it to its destination. This plane, along with another from Boston crashed into the World Trade Center, at 8:45 A.M. and 9:03 A.M., respectively, according to the Boston Globe. Dark smoke hovered throughout lower Manhattan like a big blanket covering what was a blue sky on a wonderful morning. At 10 A.M. the first tower came tumbling down like a domino piece and at 10:30 A.M. the second tower fell as well leaving onlookers in horrid disbelief. The Globe reported that "chaos broke out when the first building collapsed, some people were even abandoning their cars in the middle of the streets. People were screaming and praying to God." Numerous people are dead and the number of dead has not completely been counted. As you will note, I am trying to complete a book, but God is completing a chapter.

What occurred on this day reminds me of the book of Revelation when the Sixth Seal was opened. John writes in Revelation 6:12-17, ***"and I beheld when he had opened the sixth seal, and, lo, there was a great earthquake; and the sun became black as sackcloth of hair, and the moon became as blood. And the stars of heaven fell unto the earth, even as a fig tree casteth her untimely figs, when she is shaken of a mighty wind. And the heaven departed as a scroll when it is rolled together; and every mountain and island were moved out of their places. And the kings of the earth, and the great men, and the rich men, and the chief captains, and the mighty men, and every bondman, and every free man, hid themselves in the dens, and in the rocks of the mountains; And said to the mountaions and rocks, Fall on us, and hide us from the face of him that sitteth on the throne, and from the wrath of the Lamb: For the great day of his wrath is come; and who shall be able to stand? (Rev. 6:12-17)***

When Manhattan was hit, the people in and around the scene felt as if they were experiencing their last day. The Boston Globe described the scene as follows: "Chunks of rubble lay in the street. Everywhere, there was thick, white, ankle-deep dust, like volcanic ash. As it coated cars, trees, and bushes-and the faces of survivors still struggling northward from the blast-the scene had an erie winter quality, as if

Manhattan had been hit by a freak September snowstorm. Several cars near the Trade Center erupted in flame, as did nearby gas lines. On West Street more than 50 police officers and fire fighters struggled to put out small fires while also trying to rescue those trapped in the building when it collasped."

Never have I seen a time when the city that never sleeps shut down, with virtually no one walking the streets of New York City, and signs saying "New York City closed," posted everywhere. The landmark Twin Towers of New York's World Trade Center was hit, and a third plane crumpled part of the Pentagon. Four Aircrafts have been taken over, and never has the United States witnessed anything like this before. Everyone is saying it is time to pray; however, it has never been time not to pray. I witnessed on the news people jumping out of buildings with their spouses, and many other persons covered in debris from the World Trade Center. Firemen tried relentlessly to do their job of saving others, but to no avail as the buildings of the World Trade Center came collapsing on them, ending their lives. I heard a reporter say, as she was trying to do her job, that a fire ball from one of the buildings came down in her direction. A fireman who happened to be there, scooped her up, and slammed her into a building covering her from the fire. She recalls that she could feel his heart pumping rapidly.

All of this is more proof that we are living in the last days. This lets me know that we need to fast and seek the face of God continuously, for tomorrow is not promised to any man. I heard people screaming for their lives, and it was as though the book of Revelation was coming to pass. Many people felt as though the world was coming to an end. Thus, 911- It's a state of emergency.

Our condolences truly go out to the families of those lost in these great tradgedies. Many churches have been opened for prayer today, but the Lord has already told us that it is time to redeem the times.

For no man knows the day, neither the hour when the Lord will come. It is clear that we must always be on guard. We should never stop completely fasting and praying. Several people called me today, and told me their churches were opened for prayer. I believe the church should always be available for those that desire to pray, not only when tradgedy occurs. Let us stay on guard, and remember, if you want to dial the right number to God, it is a state of emergency, 911.

Apostle. Dr. P.W. Reed, Ph.D.

P.W. Reed, Ph.D. is a driven leader with 34 years of experience working in private and non-private sectors. He earned dual degrees at Cambridge College in education and psychology. He earned his doctoral degree in Education with a focus on Adult learning and business management from Walden University. Dr. Reed earned his clinical license as a therapist in Boston, MA., where he provided treatment and support to level 1-3 sexual offenders, athletes and families in healthy living. He is the CEO of Five Stars Empowerment Motivational Speaking company, former CEO of a Substance and Drug abuse center that provided crisis intervention, marriage and family therapy, mental health treatment, preventative health and personal training.

He is sought out as and Motivational speaker serving: Instructors, business professionals conducting effective team building skills, sales training and inspirational lecturing to sales organizations, business executives, college students and staff. He is the author of "The Impact of Self-Efficacy on Retention in Technical Colleges" which is circulated in seven countries and used for research among master's level and doctoral students.

He has authored books titled, "10 Things Every Lady and Man Needs from One Another". Additionally, he is currently publishing "The Power of Fasting and Prayer", "Mastering Team Building", and "KISS (keep it Simple Salesperson), and "Advising Made Simple".

Dr. Reed has been the Executive Director of several colleges and managed in excess of 300 employees nationally. He also served as a Senior Sales Director, Marketing Director and consultant for four beauty colleges, technical colleges, and vocational schools in Florida,

Boston, Rhode Island, Texas, Nevada and Atlanta, GA. In addition, his career has taken him to a place consulting with colleges and private businesses as trainer, coach, and instructional/ curriculum developer. He had taken colleges on the verge of closing to a high performing institutions that had the lowest attrition in the nation's highest graduation rate, and exceeded marketing quotas by 200%. Additionally

Dr. Reed has also worked as a philanthropist serving non-profit organizations and has seeded over $100,000 Trinidad, Jamaica, West Africa, and Haiti.

www.ingramcontent.com/pod-product-compliance
Lightning Source LLC
Chambersburg PA
CBHW051837090426
42736CB00011B/1841